TR

Eric Johns .... e
fictionalized background to several of his books,
including *Trip of a Lifetime*. Before settling
down to write, he lived for a time in France. He
has worked as a bank clerk, soldier, grape-
picker, interpreter, taxi driver, postman, civil
servant and salesman, and excuses his varied CV
by claiming that a writer needs wide experience.
When not writing, he divides his time between
watchkeeping in a cliff-top lookout and beach-
combing with his dog. Married with three
children, he is the author of several stories for
children and young adults, including *Capture by
Aliens!*, *My Life as a Movie Hero* and *After the
End of the World*.

Books by the same author

After the End of the World

My Life as a Movie Hero

For younger readers

Capture by Aliens!

TRIP OF A LIFETIME

ERIC JOHNS

WALKER BOOKS
AND SUBSIDIARIES
LONDON · BOSTON · SYDNEY

First published 2000 by Walker Books Ltd
87 Vauxhall Walk, London SE11 5HJ

This edition published 2001

2 4 6 8 10 9 7 5 3 1

Text © 2000 Eric Johns
Cover design © 2000 Walker Books Ltd

The right of Eric Johns to be identified as author
of this work has been asserted by him in accordance
with the Copyright, Designs and Patents Act 1988.

This book has been typeset in Sabon

Printed in Great Britain by
Cox & Wyman Ltd, Reading, Berkshire

British Library Cataloguing in Publication Data:
a catalogue record for this book is
available from the British Library.

ISBN 0-7445-7863-9

CONTENTS

INTRODUCING ME – SEX MANIAC

All this happened to me last summer. I really lost it. It was like I'd blown every circuit in my head. Things were off the wall. That's why I want to write it all down honestly, just as it happened.

What I did was, I stole a wad of money while I was on holiday, then I tried to commit suicide but I ended up killing a girl instead.

I said I wanted to be honest, but I've already told a sort of lie. I'm always doing this, even when I know I'll be found out and have to climb down. I twist something because it sounds better. So it's not my idea to be honest; it's my psychiatrist's. She says I've got to look at what happened to me and see how it's all part of my reality. Whatever. I bet she says that to all the boys. Anyway, rehabilitation's the name of the game.

Mum was on her third used car salesman. I mean, she'd been married three times since my dad. They weren't really used car salesmen, but they were the sort who flashed their money about and asked to have it nicked. Which is what I did.

When Mum brought Jake home he tried to be matey and asked what I wanted to do when I left school. It was obvious all he was doing was putting on a won't-I-make-a-great-father act for Mum.

I said, dead serious, "I want to be a used car salesman."

"You've never mentioned that before, Michael," Mum said, not getting what I was on about but shifting effortlessly into interested-parent mode.

"The boy's got his head screwed on all right, Doris," Jake said, laying down the law and giving me a wink to let me know I'd have an ally in the home from now on. "There's money in that game." He rubbed his thumb and fingers together.

Those were things which really irritated me. The way he put actions to what he said as if you were too dumb to understand words, and kept repeating people's names because he thought everyone should be flattered to hear themselves mentioned by him.

It's funny how people keep on doing the same thing – like a nervous twitch. I do it by exaggerating and climbing down. Mum does it by marrying the same person over and over. You'd have thought one Jake was enough for anyone, but now she was blithely trying to make what had failed twice work with Jake III – her third shithouse.

(That's one of my obscure puns.) Watching Mum was like watching a hamster running in its wheel.

I haven't mentioned my dad, husband number one. Well, I did, just in passing, but it sounded better to say that I hadn't.

He's done the same as Mum. Married the same person again, only an American version. That's where he lives, in the States.

I've been there several times for holidays since he left. He's filthy rich. Owns a transport company with a fleet of rigs which "covers the whole eastern seaboard". That's how his adverts describe it. It really is a big operation. He's got depots in all the major cities and Canada.

His wife is called Lois. She's dark and not very tall, like Mum and me. When I'm over there, people who see us together often think we're related. She comes from the South and has one of those suck-you-off voices.

She says things like, "Yo-all jus' make yo'self at home, y'hear?" When I was a kid I used to get the giggles when she said "yo-all" as though there were half a dozen of me.

Dad's been married to her for as long as I can remember, not like Mum. Perhaps he thinks that if you're going to marry the same person each time, there's not much point in changing. More likely, Lois knows when she's on to a good thing and doesn't aim to let him go.

They've got loads of money, like I said, and they're not tight with it either. What they keep doing is explaining what they think about it. Most Americans seem to do this and Dad's picked it up. It's funny at first, a bit embarrassing, but you get used to it.

Each time I go there Dad says, "Just because it didn't work out between your mom and me, that's no reason to think I bear her any ill-will. We don't want you or your mom to go short of anything. When I say 'we', I mean Lois and me. We both feel the same. Isn't that so, Lois?"

"That's right, honey."

"So if you're in need of anything just you write and let us know. We're open-handed folk. You remember that."

"Never mind about writing. Jus' pick up that ol' telephone and call collect, y'hear? Yo' daddy's the mos' kind-hearted man I know, that's why I upped and married him, and he won't let yo' or yo' momma suffer."

Besides drawling in that sexy voice, she always looks straight at you, inviting. Last time I was over there things really got out of hand.

On the day I arrived, Lois came up to my bedroom with me. I was jet-lagged after the journey, and it was steaming hot. The air-conditioning had packed up and there were men in the basement fixing it. I planned to have a cold shower and unpack. But she started on her welcome speech.

"Yo' jus' make yo'self right at home, y'hear?" she told me, standing closer than necessary.

"While yo're here I'm going to be yo' Dixie momma. So anything yo' want yo' jus' go right ahead and holler."

While she was saying this she was pushing her breasts towards me – at least, I thought she was – inviting me to get an eyeful, which wasn't difficult as they were not small and were bursting out of her blouse. It was so tight I could see the outline of her bra, which was one of those bottom-half-only ones. The top buttons were undone, so I could see her breasts pushing up trying to get out. I thought it would need only one more button undone for them to escape.

Just as I was thinking this she started twiddling with the buttons on my shirt and flattening down the material.

"While yo're here I'm going to treat yo' like my own baby. Yo're not too big to need looking after."

It seemed to me that while she was saying this, her breasts started to squirm about all by them-selves, like kittens struggling to get out of a sack. It must have been the heat, a mirage, like in the desert. It gets really hot there and I was sweating by this time.

"Anything yo' want, yo' jus' help yo'self or ask yo' momma." It sounded like an invitation.

That was when the hallucination happened.

I saw myself stretch out a sweaty hand and start fiddling with her buttons, as she was with mine, and begin popping them undone. Her expression turned to one of horror as she realized she was in the presence of a sexual degenerate. She screamed. The sound was still echoing in my ears when there was the thudding of Timberland boots on the stairs and the workmen from the basement burst in.

Then I blinked and realized with relief it had been a hallucination, but afterwards I kept thinking, what if I'd really done that? It had seemed so real. I kept imagining the headline, "Boy Rapes Stepmother", and I became terrified that one day a hallucination would take over and I'd wake up to find I'd really done something crazy.

Just in time I changed my gesture towards her and instead of popping her buttons I wiped my forehead. The whole scene was probably dead innocent to her and she didn't mean a thing by it. Certainly not what I thought. It's difficult enough normally knowing what a girl wants, let alone guessing what a woman almost as old as your mother and in another country wants you to do. It wouldn't sound very convincing trying to explain it was all a misunderstanding. They give you about nine hundred years down there for messing about with their women, if they don't lynch you first.

Then she repeated, "Yo' jus' ask momma," and I blurted out, "How old are you?" Just like that, because I couldn't think of what else to say and I felt I'd got to say something or my hallucination might take over. It's one of those times that makes me cringe.

"Yo' sho' are the cutest little thing," she

12

exclaimed, patting my cheek and getting even closer. "Hereabouts we never ask a lady her age. But I'll tell yo'." Then she pulled my head down like she was going to breast-feed me and whispered, "I'm thirty-five and that's where I'm staying." I could feel her breath in my ear and I was on the point of exploding.

I wondered afterwards if I was cursed like Oedipus. He was this mixed-up Greek guy who married his mother. At least he had the excuse of not knowing who she was. I should warn you that I'm into myths. My psychiatrist is as well. More of that later.

I still don't know what Lois really wanted. The trouble is, I'm obsessed by sex. Not that it's surprising, given my parents.

Look at it this way. Dad's married a nymphomaniac, and Mum polishes off husbands the way a monkey polishes off bananas. With that DNA it's not surprising that all I think about is sex, and that I keep interpreting the most innocent remarks as having hidden sexual meanings. That's what I do all the time, like with Lois. And the looks Dad gives her when she walks away wiggling her arse could be perfectly innocent too, I suppose. Well, I don't think it's *all* me, that's all.

I hadn't intended to go on about my parents and this sex thing, but it's probably as well that I did, as I think it's the cause of a lot of my problems.

I'll give you an example of how degenerate I am. I know that if there was a terrorist bomb, I wouldn't rush up to help, but to see if any woman's skirt had been torn off.

That's me – sex maniac.

THE LAST SUPPER

What I started out to tell you about was this mad time I had last summer. It began when we were at The Cottage. Mum always seems to talk about it in capital letters.

She says things like, "I simply must nip down to The Cottage this weekend or I'll collapse." I've never known anyone else get knackered going to the hairdresser's, which is about all she does during the week. Except for the sex stuff with Jake which messes up her hair in the first place.

This cottage was the result of the divorce from Jake I. I was quite young then and didn't know that divorce could be profitable. So when Mum told me that Jake had gone away on business and wouldn't be living with us anymore and that he'd given us this cottage at the seaside as a goodbye present, I swallowed it all.

It's a converted fisherman's cottage. That is, it's two cottages knocked into one with an ornamental railing round it, central heating, deep freeze, double glazing, satellite dish, fax, e-mail and a third cottage turned into a garage. The only thing connected with fishing is a wrought-iron outline of a lobster-pot screwed on the wall by the door. There's also Jake's motor launch moored in the bay. Mum always says what a relief it is to get back to the simple life.

Last summer when we came to The Cottage it was for me to relax after doing my GCSE exams. Mum made them sound as strenuous as going to the hairdresser's. I didn't think I'd done very well because I've got this terrible problem with concentrating. Everything turns into sex. For instance, when I was revising the Second World War, I started to imagine I was Hitler and how I could just snap my fingers and have any girl I fancied.

I'm ashamed of myself daydreaming things like this and I try to stop, but another part of me sort of puts on the video in my head before I know what's happening. In spite of this, I did brilliantly in my exams and got about twenty starred A's. (That's a bit of an exaggeration, in case you hadn't realized.)

All our group had done well. Especially Theo, which didn't surprise me. He's my best mate. Although we're so different, we get on really well. It's one of those relationships where one of us only has to say about half a sentence for the other to understand what he's getting at. Theo agonizes over everything while I have this suicidal urge to shatter the world by acting without thinking.

Last summer was supposed to be a break before starting my A levels.

"Give you a chance to decide what you want to do next," Jake told me as the car stopped at The Cottage.

I didn't take much notice of that casually dropped remark because as far as I was concerned everything was supposed to have been decided already. I'd chosen my courses for next term in the sixth form and even knew which universities I was going to apply for. I plan to be a lawyer.

But Jake had different ideas. What they were I learned that night when I heard him selling them to Mum.

What is it about a change of beds that makes people sexy? I'd noticed it with Jake II as well. First night at The Cottage and it was always bim-bam, thank you, ma'am. Not that Mum wasn't as bad.

That night, as usual, Mum had too much to drink and got giggly. I was just thinking it was about time she went all coy, when she yawned. "Bedtime, I think," she said innocently. "The journey's made me sleepy."

"Not too sleepy, I hope," Jake replied with a leer.

"Jake!" Mum giggled, glancing in my direction to remind him that I was there.

"Mike's too young to understand," Jake told her while winking at me.

What I thought I'd like to do was superglue his eyelids. His winking was as irritating as repeating your name.

Their bedroom was next to mine. Both rooms have got these gable windows which stick up in the roof. It was a hot night so the windows were open about an arm's length apart.

The first thing I heard were bedsprings as someone got into bed. It's one of those big old brass ones, with legs and metal springs. In my opinion, they'd been ripped off by the antique shop which had probably picked it up at the dump.

Jake's voice came through the window first. "Come on, Doris. I can't wait all night."

Then Mum's voice, all giggly: "You go ahead and start without me."

I lay on my bed with the light on and listened. I wondered whether they thought that sound travelled in straight lines and that what they said went through the window and harmlessly out across the English Channel like a beam from the lighthouse. There was some more giggling, then the clanging of unoiled springs.

"Shussh! Michael will hear," Mum whispered, more loudly than when she'd been talking. It was almost as though she wanted me to hear and understand what she was doing. That's what I remember thinking at the time, but it may have been just my obsessed way of looking at everything. Like Lois again.

"It's time the boy learnt the facts of life," Jake replied so that I could hear.

"You know I can't relax," Mum complained.

Jake muttered something, probably swore. I would have if I'd been in his position.

I got off my bed, turned out the light and stuck my head through the window to get some cool night air. The stone roofs of other cottages descended like steps towards the sea. Between two of them I could see blackness which flickered with reflected light from the streetlamps, and I could hear a rhythmic slapping on wet sand.

I was just beginning to daydream about a life of my own as a simple lobster fisherman, the way I used to when I was a kid, when Jake's voice suddenly polluted the view.

"You know, Doris," Jake said thoughtfully, "Michael's old enough to be living his own life. He shouldn't be hanging round your neck at his age."

"We can't do anything about that," Mum replied. "He's only sixteen. You'll just have to put up with things, like you agreed."

"When I agreed, I didn't know the little puppy was going to be in bed with us."

Their voices were so clear, I looked to see whether they were leaning out of the window next to me. It was wide open, but only their words were floating through.

Then Mum giggled and I thought they were ready to get on with it. Instead, Jake started talking again, this time in a reasoned tone. It sounded as though he'd got the speech all prepared.

"Seriously, Doris. It would be good for him – for all of us – if he could be a bit more independent."

"Well, I don't see how…"

"Now let me finish. I've been giving this some thought, so don't dismiss it out of hand, Doris." Jake paused for effect. "Michael wants to stay on at school to do these A level things. Right?" I nodded. "Not my cup of tea, but live and let live, I always say."

"Hear, hear," I echoed him.

"What I was thinking was this. Suppose we get him into a sixth form boarding school. It would cost a bob or two, but we're not short of the ready, and it would be money well spent. You'd be more yourself and Michael would have a chance to stand on his own two feet."

"Cunning bastard," I exclaimed admiringly.

"Don't say anything right away. You sleep on it."

The bedsprings began to squeak in a thoughtful way.

That was when I had another of my hallucinations. It was so real I was convinced that it was happening.

"I want a say in this," I announced to the night air, and climbed out the window onto the roof.

I shuffled along towards their room with my toes in the gutter and my fingers clawing at the rough edges of the stone flags that covered the roof. It never entered my head that I could fall.

I reached their window, swung myself round the casement and poked my head in.

"OK if I join you?" I asked.

There was a surprised clang of bedsprings and my foot slipped. I shot backwards. My hands were already on the windowsill so I grabbed wildly at it and hung on.

"I'll get him!" Jake cried, leaping out of bed.

His face appeared above me. "Here's my hand," he told me. His fingers covered my face and dug into my eyes.

I gave a yell, my fingers uncurled and I fell backwards. Until that moment I'd completely forgotten about the spiked railings below.

I yelled "Aaah!" as I felt my back transfixed by the spikes. It was a second before I realized that I was still inside my own room.

I was just feeling relieved when echoing "Aaahs!" came from the other window.

I thought of giving a round of applause or knocking on the wall and asking if anyone was sick apart from me. But I remained draped over the sill and listened to the sea.

I thought of my old idea of being a fisherman. It was still attractive, though I knew I couldn't be. I think I was trying to comfort myself by thinking about a time when life had seemed simpler. I also used to dream of being a smuggler. Jake's launch would be ideal for bringing stuff ashore. The customs never know where you've been unless you tell them. The system's an invitation to smuggling. But drugs are about the only thing worth smuggling these days and I disapprove of them. Well, sometimes I do. To be honest, it depends on my mood.

In the end I went to bed without any ideas about how to scupper Jake's plans for winkling me out of the happy home.

Hearing people screwing next door to you makes you hot yourself, so I started imagining being a smuggler of Asian refugees, and the modestly giggling girls with downcast eyes were so grateful at being brought to these shores that all they wished for was the opportunity to show their gratitude in the only way they knew.

"Racist sex maniac," I sighed contentedly, and fell asleep.

Jake's proposals for getting rid of me were brought up over supper the next evening. Like salmonella.

"It's a week since you finished school," Jake began casually, with his mouth full. "Have you been giving some thought to your future?"

"Thought?" I replied, frowning, as though I hadn't expected to hear the word on his lips.

"About what you're going to do, dear," Mum explained.

I used the deliberate misunderstanding approach, which is a favourite of mine. "I'd still like to be a used car salesman," I said modestly, as though confessing to an overambitious dream.

"I thought you wanted to do these A levels." Jake sounded irritated.

"I do, yes."

"You don't need certificates to sell cars."

"The careers teacher says," I began in an innocent voice, "that qualifications for all jobs are going up all the time. Really, to sell used cars you need a degree in mechanical engineering, and after that, to be on the safe side, a diploma in business studies. Then there's a course in dress sense and body language so you can spot a mug when you see one. Then…"

Even they could see I was taking the piss.

"He's trying to live up to his name," Jake sneered, showing his irritation. I noticed Mum blink as she made the effort of remembering that Dad's and my surname was Jester.

Jake took a deep breath. "If you won't be serious, you can't expect us to help you," he whined, looking to Mum for support.

I could see what was going to happen. They'd nag me into losing my temper, then I'd get the blame for not being reasonable and falling in with Jake's plans.

"My courses for next year are all arranged," I said shortly.

"We thought you might like a change from that school," Mum said. "A private residential sixth form college." She sounded like a travel agent trying to sell a holiday on a sewage farm. I wondered at what point last night she'd thought of that seductive title for it.

"Sounds like a home for delinquents," I commented.

"Be reasonable, dear…"

"Reasonable, shmeasonable."

23

"It's no use, Doris. He's determined to be child-ish," Jake said, crudely trying another tack.

"Be honest," I suggested.

"What do you mean?" Mum put on her devoted-mother's-only-wish-is-to-understand-her-trying-offspring expression.

"You just want me out of the way so that you can screw at full volume."

"Apologize to your mother!" Jake demanded, turning purple. I thought he was going to have a stroke, but no such luck.

"I apologize," I said in a contrite voice. "I'll buy some earplugs."

"Oh, Michael..."

I got up quickly and walked out, without slamming the door.

I heard Jake saying, "Let him go, Doris. We've all been young and hotheaded. I think we should go ahead and arrange a place for him at this college. He just needs time to come round to our way of seeing things..."

I thought of going back and saying I'd need my brain amputated before I saw things his way.

I didn't really feel angry or anything. I'd only walked out for effect, but I decided it would be my last meal with them until they surrendered.

I thought I'd go out for the evening to give myself time to think. My half-eaten supper would stare at them accusingly. I took a couple of twenties from Mum's handbag in passing, in case I got hungry.

HOW NOT TO
GET DRUNK

After my exit I wasn't sure what I was going to do.
I was pretty pissed off by the way Mum had
betrayed me, but I felt more depressed than angry.

It wasn't dark yet, so I went down to the
seafront, which was cluttered with holidaymakers,
and ambled along in an aimless way waiting for an
opportunity to be heroic which, as usual, didn't
happen.

In order to watch a girl in a café, I stopped and
pretended to look at a rack of postcards. The girl
threw herself back in her chair, laughing like mad
at something her friend had said. She was obviously
overreacting because she knew I was watching her.
That made me lose interest and I started glancing at
the postcards.

There was one which showed a seaside promenade being lashed by rain and spray, and some
miserable people in a shelter. The words were,
Wish you were here. That really amused me. It still

does for some reason.

Another showed this couple in four pictures. In one they were gazing into each other's eyes. In the second there was a small child between them, but they were still looking at each other. In the third there were two children between them and the girl was looking at them, while the man still looked at her. In the last there were three children and the girl was watching them while the man looked at a girl in a bikini. I thought that was pretty funny too, in a bitter sort of way.

There was one other card I remember. This just showed a couple in bed. The man was smoking and looking bored, and the woman was lying there talking and bricks were flying out of her mouth and building a wall between them. I didn't think this was funny. For some reason it made my stomach lurch and I felt like crying for the sadness of everything. I didn't, of course, and it was only for a moment. I don't understand why it had that effect, but it was one of the reasons for what happened later. Because I decided then that I'd get drunk, which is why I mention it.

I've only been drunk twice before. Once was after a school disco when I acted worse than I was to get a big reputation. The other time was at Mum's wedding to Jake III. I enjoyed it both times, until later in the night when I lay down and everything went round and I was sick.

I wanted to get away from holidaymakers, so I went up a cobbled alleyway to a pub I'd noticed a few times but never been in. It looked dingy and unattractive, which was why I chose it. There was just one door, like for an ordinary house, and a dark, sloping corridor. I supposed that it led to the bar but it was so long that I couldn't see.

The outside wall was a dirty cream colour, the door was navy blue or black and the name, which was painted on the wall, was peeling off. It was called The Jolly Sailor, which was a laugh, as you'll see.

I groped my way down the corridor. It was very narrow and made worse because all along one side were stacks and stacks of chairs, thick with dust. There must've been thousands. About halfway along I wondered if I'd made a mistake and come in the back way and there was another entrance I'd never noticed.

The corridor turned right at the bottom and in front of me was the bar. It was almost as dark as the corridor and the same width, with the bar itself taking the place of the chairs. A line of four men sat on bar stools, hunched over pint glasses, straight ones. They all fell silent and turned to stare at me like a press-gang which has spotted a likely victim. They wore roll-neck navy pullovers, heavy twill jackets and were obviously not holidaymakers.

I can usually pass for eighteen in that sort of light so, in spite of the cool reception, I tried to walk casually up to the bar.

A bald and greasy barman who looked like an

ex-wrestler winked at his regulars, then raised himself to look over my shoulder at some imaginary object in the corridor. What is it about me that attracts people with dodgy eyelids?

"I'm sorry, sir," he said. "Fire regulations. Can't leave them there."

"What?" I asked, keeping it short.

"Not allowed to block the corridor." He paused. "They are yours, aren't they?"

"What?" I asked, repeating my impression of a man of few words since it had gone down so well the first time.

"That bucket and spade. I did see you put it there, didn't I, sonny?"

His customers were loving this. A regular cabaret act, as far as they were concerned.

"You must be the jolly sailor mentioned outside," I said, ignoring his remark. No one thought that was funny. "A pint of bitter, please."

"What're you planning to do with it, sonny?"

"Wash my feet in it," I told him. It was obvious he wasn't going to serve me so I didn't have anything to lose. "If the rest of this place is anything to go by, it won't be fit to drink."

One of the customers drew in his breath with a whistling sound. "We got a connosewer of beer here, Jo," he said, shaking his head.

"Beat it, sonny," the barman said. He made it include a threat of physical violence. "Men only, here."

I looked him up and down. "Mmm, is that so?"

I said. "You could have fooled me." I tried to make it sound as though I'd taken him to be gay.

I've nothing against gays, but I guessed he'd be outraged at any suggestion that he was one. Anyway, it was the best I could think of at the time. I flicked my eyebrows at him and turned to go.

Before I reached the door, which was only two steps away, a huge wet dishcloth hit me in the middle of my back and soaked my shirt with stale beer.

"Thrown in the towel, have you?" I don't know why I said that, except I was furious and it was the first thing which came into my head. Just because they're decrepit, they think they can say what they like and treat you any way. Not to mention arrange your life for you.

Then I had one of my hallucinations. At least, I thought I did.

"You want to throw things?" I yelled. "OK. Here you are, then."

I picked up the bar stool propping the door open and hurled it at the barman. He stepped sideways instead of catching it, which was a mistake, as it smashed into a row of spirit bottles behind him.

A couple of regulars slid off their stools like snakes gliding off branches in a rainforest.

Suddenly, I realized that this time it wasn't a hallucination. I'd really done it.

I was so surprised that for a second I was frozen. Then I fled.

The corridor in front of me looked endless. It

was like one of those nightmares where you're being chased by something merciless and you know you'll never get away. Only this time it was for real and my fate was no more than two paces behind me. I could already feel them kicking me in the balls.

Then inspiration hit me: the chairs. As I passed, I pulled down stack after stack. The whole corridor became a mass of chair legs knitted together. It would take hours to clear.

The street door was opened flat against the corridor wall and I noticed that the key was on the inside. Calmly, I took it out, shut the door and locked it. Distantly I could hear voices swearing.

I was just congratulating myself on keeping my cool when the thought that there might be another way out recurred, and with it the vision of a posse of regulars appearing round the corner. I ran down to the seafront and mingled with the holidaymakers. It was still not quite dark and the contrast between these peaceful evening strollers with their whining kids and the trolls I'd just escaped was dizzying.

I leaned over the promenade railings and stared at the sea. I found I was trembling. It was not the shock of nearly being mauled by the Jolly Sailor's gorillas, but the fact that a hallucination had taken over.

I suppose I'd better tell you honestly about these hallucinations.

They'd started out with me imagining things.

Like what I ought to have said in an argument. You know the sort of thing. You've been humiliated by some guy you hate and the scene keeps going round in your head until you've thought of the perfect reply that would have demolished him. Then you repeat it over and over until you almost believe that was what you said.

That's OK. Everyone does it. But then I started imagining things I'd like to happen. For example, while I was clinging to the railings getting over my narrow escape and letting my shirt dry, I spotted Jake's boat moored a little way out in the bay. That started off a hallucination I'd had before about getting rid of him. Hallucinations automatically adjust themselves to the latest developments. So that evening's version included Jake's plans for getting shot of me.

I saw myself returning to The Cottage and talking man to man.

"Jake, I think I owe you an apology. No, don't say anything. Let me finish. I realize you were only thinking of what was best for all of us as a family, and I was only thinking of myself. So let me say that I'd be happy to fall in with your suggestion."

"Oh, I knew you'd come round to our way of thinking," Mum exclaims.

"You're a good lad, Mike. I always said so," Jake confesses. "Now. I tell you what. We'll leave your mum to clear up and we'll take the boat out of the bay and really open her up. See what she can do. What d'you say?"

Sometime later I stagger back to The Cottage dripping wet.

"Mum, I've got some news about Jake," I announce in a choked voice. "You'd better sit down."

Mum's hand flies to her throat.

"Jake was thrown overboard when we hit the tide race. I went back to try to find him but, by a bit of bad luck, I chopped him up with the propeller."

"I just knew things were going too well to last." She sighs. "Still, look on the bright side. He'd changed his will in my favour."

"That's the spirit, Mum. Plenty more Jakes in the sea." Well, there are by the sewage outfall.

That sort of hallucination was OK too. Because it was so far-fetched, I knew even while it was going on it wasn't real. The ones that worried me were those I didn't know were hallucinations until afterwards. Like with Lois.

What I was scared of was that one time I'd wake up and find that it had not been a hallucination but that I'd really done it. Whatever it was. Now it had happened. You might say, forget it, no harm done except for a few broken bottles and the trolls deserved that. But think about it. What if it had been the time with Lois and I'd torn her blouse off. It wouldn't have sounded very convincing saying, "Oh, it wasn't me, it was a hallucination." And what about *next* time? Some of my hallucinations you could get locked up for.

I'll give you an example. Once I was on a train and it had stopped for ages in the middle of nowhere because there was a fault on the line. Well, I suddenly imagined myself unzipping my flies and saying to everyone in the carriage, "You don't mind if I pull myself off to pass the time, do you?"

Well, I said I'd be honest. So what d'you expect from a sex maniac? But just suppose I'd done that? Nightmare. Men in white coats. Loony bin. Now you can see why I was scared stiff.

But here's the creepy bit: at the same time I *wanted* to lose control. A treacherous part of me was on the hallucinations' side, because afterwards nothing would ever be the same again. I'd have shattered my world.

I leaned on the railings and breathed deeply until I felt calmer, then jumped down onto the sand and threw the key to The Jolly Sailor as far out to sea as I could. After that I suddenly felt great.

You probably think that chucking a key in the sea would not be enough to change anyone's mood from depressed to hyper. I agree. But that's what happens with me. My life's an emotional seesaw.

I decided to go to The Grey Mare, which was the pub I usually used, and get drunk like I'd originally planned. It was better than most pubs because there was an upstairs bar with music that hadn't been on a cruise with Noah. I'd been going there since I was thirteen, when I used to tell Mum I went to the café. No one bothered about your age. In any case, you were lucky if you ever got served because the bargirls spent all their time looking in the mirror behind the optics.

We came down to The Cottage often enough out of season for me to know a few people. This was the gathering place for trapped local kids when everything else closed down for the winter.

In spite of the crush of holidaymakers one of the first people I saw was Ade. He's a couple of years older than me and one of those characters who's been middle-aged since he was five. I met his father once and when I wasn't looking I couldn't tell who was speaking. They not only sounded the same but said the same sort of thing. Anyway, Ade's loud and insensitive as only someone whose dad owns a boatyard that builds Jake-type launches can be. As a result he has loads of confidence, and in spite of everything I've just said, I quite like him.

"Mike!" He greeted me like a long-lost brother returned from the antipodes. "The very man I was hoping to see."

"Liar," I said. He didn't hear me because of the music. Not that it would have mattered, Ade wasn't the sensitive type.

"You'll have to shout."

"Pint of bitter," I shouted.

"That's what I like to hear," he said. "Hold these." He gave me two half-pint glasses with stems, which suggested to my lightning-swift GCSE-trained brain that he had two girls in tow and wanted to offload one of them.

Ade's quite big and he shoved himself back to the bar, where he leant over someone so that he got served first, no doubt booming something about forgetting his granny's bitter. No one seems to mind being trampled on by him, I've noticed.

"Here you are!" he shouted, returning. "Let me put you in the picture." At this convenient moment the music took a break. I could see that life would always be like that for Ade, falling over itself to fit in with his smallest need. One of the bargirls had turned the sound down so that she could explain to a holidaymaker that it was a Grey Mare tradition to overcharge and if the punter didn't like it he could sup at The Jolly Sailor.

"I've got these two student nurses stashed away in a corner. On holiday, looking for a bit of fun. Nudge-nudge, wink-wink, know what I mean? Yours is darkish. The small one," he said generously.

"Are we talking bust measurements?"

"Got it in two," he said, and had a quick pull at his glass. "Called Anna or Karen. Didn't get which name belonged to which. Fifty percent chance of being right."

"Nurses," I repeated.

He winked. "Know what you're thinking."

I wished I did.

Ade pushed his way through the crowd as though he was wading out to sea. Bodies eddied round him. I tried to move in his wake. Eventually we arrived and I slopped some beer on the blonde girl in greeting.

"This is Mike," Ade shouted. "You'll have to watch him."

"I can see that," the blonde said, mopping herself up. But she glanced up to smile so that it didn't sound sharp or bitchy, and at the same time made it clear that she was taking Ade's introduction as Ade's introduction and no more. She had a lopsided smile but apart from that was quite good-looking.

"Anna, Karen," Ade said, sweeping his hand vaguely at both.

"Anna Karenina," I said to "mine". "That name rings a bell."

It obviously didn't with her. She gave a what-stone-did-this-creep-out-from grimace to her friend, not caring if I saw. She was dark, small, sharp-featured and tarty. I'd have thought she was Ade's type.

The blonde one gave me a quick grin to show she understood and moved up a bit to make room on the bench.

"Anna will do," she said.

"Anna will do what?" I asked, then passed a hand over my face as though I'd let myself down yet again. "Sorry. Adrian's catching."

Ade dropped down next to her and started twiddling with a medallion which hung round her neck and kept trying to conceal itself between her breasts – which were obviously the reason he'd gone for her instead of Karen. A big breast man is

36

our Ade. His method was to render his victim unconscious by a non-stop recitation of clichés. Yes, I was envious: the technique worked for Ade but I couldn't do it.

I decided to invest some time in Karen, not that I ever get anywhere with her type. I ran through the basic holiday dialogue about where she came from and how long she was here for. Usually this is a duologue but with Karen it was a monologue with grunts. She seemed to have missed out on the verbal foreplay unit of her socialization. I could see that as a nurse she would be ideal for patients who wanted to die peacefully.

I wondered what it was that sullen and pouty girls got out of life. Then I tried to feel sorry for her, and decided that a bit of chat about her vocation might ignite her interest.

"Do you nurse any diseases in particular?" I asked, gazing quizzically into her vacuous brown orbs.

"Is this all there is in this town?" She flicked her eyes round the bar and generously included me in the question.

"There is the club," I told her.

"What's that?"

"It's a club."

She grunted.

I felt I was getting the hang of talking to her.

"We could go there," I suggested.

I couldn't tell whether her grunt was affirmative or not, so I gulped down some beer because I'd still got this idea of getting drunk.

"D'you want another?" I asked her.

"OK."

"Anna?"

"We're both lagers. Thanks." She was obviously used to interpreting for Karen.

"Ade?"

"Good man," he said, taking his head out of Anna's T-shirt. "Told you Mike was a fast worker."

God knows what relevance that remark had to anything, but it was the sort of conversation substitute Ade could get away with.

I'd drunk my beer pretty quickly, which was partly this drunk thing and also so that I could get the next lot in while everyone had some left. My theory was that people were less likely to notice how long I took to force my way to the bar if they were still drinking. It saved remarks like, "Been hop-picking?" or "Thought you were having it off with the barmaid".

I bought Ade his bitter, the girls their lagers and I got myself a pint of Scrumpy because it was the strongest drink in the place. When I handed over the cash I said a silent thank you to Mum and Dad or Jakes I to III: whoever she'd conned into forking out this slice of alimony. (I'm pretty well up in divorce law and from time to time I toy with the idea of being a divorce lawyer – unmarried, of course.)

When I got back to the corner, Ade had disappeared, presumably to the bog. He goes more than

38

anyone else I've ever known. You'd think it would cramp his style, but he just comes back and carries on where he left off. I drank half my Scrumpy in one go and things looked brighter.

"I'd smack my lips if I knew how," I told both the girls. I can always tell when my inhibitions are starting to lift because I can come out with inconsequential rubbish like Ade. "Things are looking brighter," I added.

"Your eyes aren't as wide open either," Anna said. She'd got a lot of little lines at the side of hers which made her expression change very rapidly.

"That's my seductive look," I explained.

"Oh, I'm sorry. I hadn't realized," she said, pretending to be concerned.

"It works without anyone being aware of it," I said, self-mocking.

"Including you?"

"Always including me. I never understand why I'm so successful." So that I didn't sound conceited, I sagged to suggest I was one of life's victims. Some girls like to comfort failure.

"It is difficult to understand," she agreed, meaning that I wasn't going to score tonight.

"Casanova is supposed to have had some special smell that just made women helpless."

"Pheromones," Nurse Anna informed me.

"It's a bit insulting to women, isn't it?"

We went on like this, with me trying to convince Anna (and myself) that I didn't think of girls as sex objects, until Ade returned with a damp patch on his flies and burrowed back into her T-shirt.

Karen suddenly came out of her coma and asked, "Are we going, then?"

Anna was obviously used to these delayed responses because she looked at me. "What were you talking about?"

I cast my mind back to before the last few millilitres of alcohol. "The club?" I suggested.

"The club?" Anna asked Karen.

Karen stood up. Her glass was already empty. It seemed she was one of those wiry girls who could drink rapidly without apparently having anywhere to stash it.

"The club it is," Ade boomed, surfacing and draping an arm round each of them.

I downed the rest of my Scrumpy but I felt sober again and, for some reason, fed up.

A SORT OF
SEASIDE ROMANCE

The club was a long, dimly lit cellar under another pub. It ripped off holidaymakers by charging them a huge amount for temporary membership, but gave away cards to locals so that the place wasn't dead in the winter. Girls could always get in free: the bouncers didn't believe in sex equality.

"Here we are," I said to Karen. "All the town's nightlife under one roof."

She studied the art round the door. Painted on the brickwork was a tropical palm tree wearing dark glasses.

"It's called Shades," I explained. "Hell of a place," I added, for the pleasure of seeing her not get the pun. All right, it's obscure, perhaps it didn't merit any reaction.

Ade and I showed our cards to the bouncers, who pretended not to know us. They had that pectoral twitch body-builders develop and seemed to be chewing oysters. They also had the necessary gorilla-length arms to stand comfortably with their hands clasped in front of their groins like footballers. They frisked Karen and Anna with their eyes and indicated the door by a minimal movement of the head. Probably not having necks made mobility difficult.

Anyone who loved clubbing would have died of grief in this place. Every night through the summer, it played twenty-year-old discs to help gross holidaymakers recover their lost youth. Looking at them, you couldn't help thinking that their youth had not been lost but fled in horror. Their T-shirts moved independently, balanced on layers of fat or mammary glands that had seen better days.

The only light came from a mirror ball pushed round by laser beams. The solid bass made the floor vibrate like a concrete trampoline. Once you were in there the outside world ceased to exist and you were absorbed into another dimension where normal rules didn't apply.

It was all an illusion. I'd seen it in the daytime once and it had looked tatty and sad. It was like any other small town club which tried to pretend it was the centre of the universe. That didn't bother Karen. She just walked in and started dancing like she'd been switched on. You could see by the way she moved that she was fantastically fit, with not a milligram of fat, and that she'd keep going until close.

There was a bar at one end and drinks cost twice

as much as in The Grey Mare, which meant that drugs were cheaper. But I was happy to allow Jakes I to III to stand us a round.

As usual, I got the drinks slowly and made my way back to Karen. I balanced a drink for her on a nearby ledge. She looked at me blankly, then, without missing a beat, pulled an enamelled pill-box out of her pocket and dropped two tablets into each of our glasses. I got the impression that this passed for social interaction with her.

"Drinka lod," I lip-read her saying, like a nurse giving good advice to a patient. I nodded obediently. After that she went into her own world.

I found myself admiring her in a funny sort of way. I was dancing next to her, but even though the beat was like a freak wave which washed over me and enveloped me and got inside my head and took me out of myself, I wasn't part of it in the way she was. She was the best dancer I'd ever seen. I couldn't move the way she did. Karen surfed the beat so perfectly she brought tears to my eyes.

I could tell, just watching her, that this was what made her life worth living. And I envied sullen, pouty Karen. She belonged somewhere and I didn't. I dropped into a trough of self-pity.

That was how I always felt, an outsider. I was in the crowd but not part of it. I drank my beer not even wondering what was in it. I'd half forgotten that there *was* anything in it, and I didn't care anyway. Because I didn't have anything. Not there, not at home, not anywhere. The seesaw was down again.

I lost track of time and dreamed as I danced.

What I dreamed of was a girl who was pure and loving and I could trust and laugh with and look after and protect and who'd love me and give me confidence and care for me and let me be weak and strong and completely myself and everything.

But all my dream did was show me how empty my life was. I felt like crying. Whatever Karen had given me didn't take my seesaw up to new heights, if that was what it was supposed to do. I went on dancing in my own private snake pit.

An immeasurable time later, I found myself looking through the wrong end of a telescope. Karen floated into view with a fresh drink. She squeezed her pill-box out of her pocket and this time seemed to drop a waterfall of coloured capsules into the glass. They looked like regular medicine, not like the stuff she'd given me. I blinked and Karen disappeared. I saw my hand casually helping itself to her drink and then going to replace the empty glass, but the ledge moved and the glass bounced on the floor before a foot kicked it away for ever. After that I was out of it.

About a century passed, then some guy who was often in the club floated in front of me. He had an ethnic sweatband round his head and mimed "Peace" at me like an ageing hippy out of a psychedelic time machine. He tore a ragged tab off some blotting-paper he was carrying and pressed it into the hollow at the base of my throat, where it was leeched to my skin by sweat. I accepted that as an example of social bonding through gift-giving (GCSE Sociology) and didn't question what it might be; which will give you some idea of how far gone I was. The bass throbbed inside me. The age of the song didn't matter any more. I hurtled along like an express and the beat came from below.

After another limitless stretch of time I became aware of a voice in my head. I stopped dancing and tried to focus my mind on what was happening. Karen was nowhere to be seen.

"Come on. Let's go." The voice had teleported out of my head and was now next to my ear.

I looked round. "Anna?"

"Let's get out of here." She held me firmly by the arm and guided me through the door. The street had emptied while we were there.

In the fresh air my head seemed to clear.

"Where're Karen and Ade?" I asked.

"Karen won't leave till the end and Ade's staying with her."

"They're together?" I asked, wondering at what point Ade had switched nurses.

"Wait till you're older, then you'll understand."

"Oh," I said, my usual brilliant repartee coming to my rescue.

"Are you all right?"

"Why did we leave?"

"You know Karen gave you something?"

I frowned. I didn't seem to be thinking too

clearly. "In your drink." I saw that she looked concerned.

"Sort of."

"She told me she'd stopped using it."

I thought slowly. "I didn't really... What was it?"

Anna shrugged. "Ecstasy, I hope. But some guy she knows has his own line in drugs and likes to experiment."

We were walking away from the club. The fresh air seemed to wake me up.

"The effect's worn off," I said.

"Tell me that again in a month's time," Anna said grimly.

Behind us the door of the club swung outwards and the bouncers ejected two middle-aged holidaymakers. The woman was mechanically beating the man with the strap of her handbag and swearing.

A window in a house opposite opened. "What's going on?" a man shouted.

"It's all right," I told him. "It's an S&M night."

Anna and I started to run. I felt a silly, giggling panic.

"I'm calling the police!" the man shouted after us, as if he hoped we'd offer to shoulder his problems.

We didn't stop until we reached the seafront, where we hung over the railings giggling uncontrollably and, in my case, feeling sick. This was where I'd ended up after leaving The Jolly Sailor. My life seemed to be going in circles.

I looked up. About a hundred metres away across the waves Jake's launch bobbed up and down, reflecting the lights from the promenade.

"That's my stepfather's," I told Anna.

She stretched out her hand towards it, fingers spread.

"What're you doing?" I asked.

"Hexing it. Turning it to stone."

"Just by being there it pollutes the bay."

"Do you feel that too?"

I nodded. "Come with me. I'll show you something." I suddenly felt completely sober.

We walked along the promenade. When we reached the old stone jetty we leaned over the wall to look at the sea.

"This jetty's been here since the town was a fishing village. It belongs." I wanted her to understand how I felt about that stupid pile of stones. "It grows out of the bay. Do you know what I mean?"

"Its stones are part of the sea and sand, like the houses in the old town."

"That's right," I agreed excitedly. "Jake's motor boat is a violation."

"This should all be for real people." She waved her arm at the sea and the dark silhouette of the cliffs.

For some reason I started to tell her about Mum and Jake and The Cottage. "It's all so pointless. Sometimes I feel like clearing off."

"Everyone feels like that at times. That doesn't mean," she added quickly, "that I think you should stay."

"I suppose we're just as bad as everyone else, with our fisherman's cottage. The locals who should live there have all moved to the new estate. They've been dispossessed by us. Intruders."

"No. You're not an intruder: you feel something genuine for the place. You don't just want the right possessions to impress people."

"When I was a kid," I said, "I just accepted that we should have a weekend cottage by the sea. Like some kids had two cars or their own computer or the latest CDs. It was simply natural, like the weather almost. I never thought that anyone might resent me and say, 'What's he done to deserve that?' Now I keep wondering if anyone feels about me the way I do about that plastic launch."

All this time we were leaning on the parapet of the jetty. Suddenly the clouds shifted and the sea became silver in the moonlight.

"I want to paddle," Anna announced.

We climbed the wall and dropped down to the beach. It became a race to get our shoes off and roll up our jeans.

Anna won. Why are girls always quicker at that sort of thing?

"It's iced moonlight!" she shrieked.

We ran along, holding hands and getting splashed. When we were breathless we staggered up the beach and flopped down on the dry sand.

"No one's going to think that about you," Anna said, going back five minutes. "It depends on the sort of person you are. If anyone thought that, they'd just be one of those people themselves. Someone who judged by appearances."

We lay and stared at the sky and watched the stars multiply. Out of sight, the waves flopped onto the sand.

"That sounds like our dog lapping its water," Anna said dreamily.

"That's just what I used to think," I exclaimed. "I imagined it was Cerberus having a drink."

"He'd make more noise than that," Anna laughed. "He had fifty heads, didn't he?"

I looked at her in surprise. "You're amazing. I've never met anyone before who's even heard of Cerberus."

"My dad used to tell me Greek myths at bedtime, as well as fairy stories. Do you know, you can't get toy dogs with more than one head? I always wanted one. Why'd Cerberus have all those heads, anyway?"

"Guard dog. Stop people getting out of hell. Or into it, I suppose. People want to do both, don't they?"

"How come you know about Cerberus then?"

"He was in this book about mythology that I had when I was a kid. On one page there was a picture of Icarus falling towards the ground with drops of wax and feathers in his slipstream. It scared me but I kept going back to it. When I looked at it I could feel the muscles in my face pulling themselves into a scream like Icarus. Somehow, I felt it was me in the picture."

"Have you hit the ground yet?"

"I'm still falling." I stared wide-eyed into the sky. "I think myths reveal archetypal truths about the human condition."

"Oooh!" she put on a sarky voice, as used by irritating tarty types if you let on you've got an IQ above double figures. "Who's swallowed a dictionary, then?"

"OK. I admit it. I read that."

"I'd never have guessed."

I rolled over and trickled fine sand through my fingers. The moon was nearly full and every grain became a minute silver star.

"Anna sounds foreign," I said.

"My dad says girls' names should end with an *a*."

"I agree with him. Though I suppose it would get a bit monotonous if they all did. It's one of those opinions you can hold so long as it's not likely to come true."

"What's the time?"

"I don't know. I left my watch when I cleared out of The Cottage."

We got up and kicked along through the sand until our feet were dry, then we climbed up on the promenade and put our shoes on. The evening had ended. We both knew it and didn't try to prolong it for fear of spoiling the future.

"It's just the right time," I said.

"That's what I feel." She took my hand and squeezed it.

Like with Theo, I only had to say half of anything and she understood all I meant.

The place she was staying was a big, red-brick guest house with garish plastic sunshades above every window.

"The Intrusion Guest House," Anna announced in an American accent like a travel film. "Bed, breakfast, evening meal and a resentful waitress."

"I'll see you again?" I said.

"Of course."

We kissed, but not to get worked up. Her lopsided mouth and the lines by her eyes stopped her being perfect.

"See you," I said.

"Do you feel all right?" she asked. "I mean, you can get home OK?"

"I'm fine now, nurse," I promised.

She gave me a worried that's-what-*you*-think look, which I paid no attention to at the time.

The front door closed and a few seconds later a light was switched on round the side of the house. I followed a path past a square bay window and saw that the light came from another room on the ground floor. I tiptoed up to it and looked in.

Anna was staring through the window at me. I jumped, then realized she was looking at her own reflection in the glass.

It crossed my mind that I seemed to spend all my nights trying to find out what went on in other people's bedrooms. It was what came of being a sex maniac, I supposed.

I knew I'd just stand there as long as I dared.

WAKING NIGHTMARE

This was when all the weird stuff began and reality crashed. At the time, I thought it was my hallucinations getting out of control. I'd forgotten about the guy with the blotting paper and about what Karen had given me and about helping myself to her drink. It turned out that Karen was the equivalent of a walking pic-'n'-mix store where the stock was supplied by the hospital pharmacy. But I can't put all the blame on her. I didn't know it at the time but I was a disaster waiting to happen. I was like a tightrope walker with a mile-long pole and Karen was just the feather that landed on one end and tipped me over Niagara.

It began with me standing outside Anna's bedroom window. Perfectly normal behaviour for a sex maniac, you say. Anna appeared to be staring straight at me. But it seemed I was invisible to her since her face was as blank as a zombie's.

She pulled off her T-shirt without a flicker of

expression. Her breasts had those large brown nipples, which surprised me, since she was fair. I'd expected little pink piglet snouts. Next she took off her jeans and pants both at the same time. She had the most startling triangle of flaming red hair, the same red as one of the laser beams at Shades.

Her expression was still blank and she was staring at me as though mesmerized. Then she began these movements, like an exercise. She reached down to her thighs and with her fingers bent like claws drew her hands up through her fur so that each hair recoiled like a delicate little spring. She continued the movement up her stomach, across her breasts and ended by extending her arms outwards above her head as though offering herself.

Every sex maniac's dream, I hear you say. But, if you can believe me, I didn't feel a bit excited because it just wasn't sexy.

She went on like this for some time until I began to feel hypnotized too. I think I even moved nearer to the window, because I noticed something that made me shudder like I'd stepped on my own grave. Behind her was a wash-basin with a mirror above it, fixed on what used to be the chimney breast. I could see the window in it and through the window I could see this ghostly outline of a face. I remember thinking, if I can see that, she must be able to see me. Then I wondered, was she doing this *for* me? Did she get a kick out of kinky exhibitionism? Nurses. Nudge-nudge, wink-wink. Know what I mean?

I looked at the mirror to share the joke with my reflection, but all that I saw was the outline of my head. There was no face. I'd vanished. I staggered back in horror and banged into a fence. This panicked me into action. I turned and ran. The empty reflection pursued me. I wasn't a real person. I'd always known it. I was nothing.

I half ran, half staggered down towards the sea. Somehow, I forgot to breathe and at the bottom of the road I had to cling to a drainpipe by a shop to stop myself collapsing. I gulped in great mouthfuls of sea air.

As my breathing slowed, I became aware of a few stragglers giving me odd looks. I turned my attention to the shop window and feigned fascination with the display. It was a TV shop. About a hundred sets were glaring at me, all showing the same picture. It was the opening montage of a news programme called *This World*. I'd seen it a few times. It was dead depressing.

The images glided from pollution, to war, to starvation, to riots, to screaming faces. Then something horrifying happened – I had a nightmare while I was awake.

The TVs hurled themselves at me and I was being crushed by black and brown bodies with sticks for limbs and distended stomachs and domed heads with all-seeing eyes and fly-encrusted mouths which were moaning something at me. I flapped my arms helplessly to fight them off. They were plucking at me and crowding closer and

closer, demanding something. I was being smoth-
ered. Their shamelessness revolted me.

Then out of the corner of my eye, I caught sight
of the old stone jetty. I knew that I had to reach it.
I fought against the crush of bodies and waded
through cloying, sewage-saturated sand towards
it. With the last of my strength, I flung myself forward and stretched out my hands. My fingertips
brushed the cool stone and, as they did, I was able
to make out what the fly-blown lips were saying to
me: "Your world, your world."

A SPOKE IN
JAKE'S WHEEL

I was cold when I woke up which wasn't surprising, as it was only just starting to get light and I'd obviously spent the night lying stark naked on the beach. I tried to remember when I'd taken off my clothes. I had a hazy impression of attempting to give them to the starving people in order to keep them at bay.

I was huddled behind one of the buttresses which support the stone jetty. This hid me from the promenade which was presumably why no late-night Peeping Tom had discovered me. I struggled up and saw my clothes lying scattered about the sand. I could hardly dress myself I was shivering so violently.

When I'd got my things on I didn't feel much better because I'd dashed out last night with only the shirt and jeans I'd worn all day. I decided to run back to The Cottage to warm myself up. That was easier to think than do. I found that I could only stagger along. I kept going by counting each step, the same as I did on cross-country runs.

It wasn't far, but it was uphill, and by the time I got there I wasn't any warmer, just out of breath. (OK, I'm understating this time.) But I was more aware of feeling sick because of the physical exertion than of being cold. I decided, while I tried to get my trembling hand to turn the door-handle, that I must get fit. (Is sex good exercise?)

Mum and Jake had left The Cottage unlocked, which was big of them since they wanted to get rid of me. But I just felt contempt because they hadn't had the nerve to lock me out and throw away the key. Since I was feeling lousy and my head was going round, I was happy to take advantage of the situation, whatever opinions I pretended to have.

I thought I'd have a soak in a hot bath. The bathroom was downstairs and at the other end of The Cottage to Mum and Jake's bedroom so there was not much danger of them waking up and giving me the benefit of their mind-numbing philosophy of life. I put the bath on and went to look at the clock in the kitchen. It wasn't even five o'clock. I helped myself to a slice of cold pizza from the fridge. Next, in quick succession, so as to save time, I was sick, had the screaming shits and a bath. I lay and soaked and sucked some toothpaste out of the tube to freshen up my mouth. Surprisingly, I found that I felt pretty good.

I must have mixed the water to about blood

temperature because I couldn't feel it unless I moved. It was like one of those sensory deprivation tanks. Once I was warm, I started to worry about last night's hallucination-cum-nightmare. Things were getting out of control. But really.

I think I drifted off to sleep at some point, because the water was suddenly cold. I levered myself out and found that my muscles had gone stiff. When I looked in the mirror I saw that I'd bruised myself down one side. God knows when I'd done that.

I dried myself and made breakfast. What was I going to do? Sit there waiting for them to get up? It would look as though I'd crept back with my tail between my legs. Jake wouldn't have much difficulty convincing Mum that the best thing for me would be to go to this borstal he'd got lined up. I had to do something to fix it so that he didn't get his way. Not that I wanted to live in the same house as him, but I wasn't going to do what he wanted. It was a matter of principle. Who did he think he was? I wondered about rat poison. Did it work on used car salesmen? Then I had a brainwave. The US cavalry!

I went and found Dad's phone number. It was still only five-thirty. About eleven-thirty at night there, I guesstimated. I dialled and got through in ten seconds flat.

"Is that Lois?"

"It sho' is," a sleepy voice told me. "Who's this?"

58

"It's Michael," I said, feeling foolish as always, saying my own name.

"Mickey, honey. Why this is jus' marvellous. Only this very mornin' I was saying to yo' daddy that he should call yo' up and say howdy."

"I'm sorry to call you so late, but something's come up."

"Don't yo' worry yo' head about the time."

"Is Dad there?"

She gave this huge moan dying away to nothing. "Oh, honey. I'm mos' terrible sorry. He flew up to Atlanta this afternoon to sort out some trouble at the depot."

"Can you give him a message for me, please? It's urgent."

"Yo' can rely on Lois. I'm yo' Dixie momma, ain't I?"

"That's right," I said, remembering her tits. "It's rather awkward this," I began, putting on the Englishness. "I don't know how to put it."

"Yo' jus' go right ahead and spit it out, as my old gran'pappy used to say."

"Well, you know that Mum got married again not long ago?"

"That's her fourth, unless I'm mistaken," she replied in a cool, southern bitch drawl that really put Mum down.

"The trouble is that Jake wants to get me out of the house. I'm in his way for some reason." Innocent little me. Let her work it out for herself. "He's planning to send me to this boarding school which is like a sort of reformatory." I used American so's she'd get the message. "I don't know what to do." I put on the helpless note to get her maternal juices flowing. (Another brief tit vision.)

"Now don't yo' worry, honey. Yo' jus' leave it all to yo' daddy and me. We'll have this sorted out in no time at all. The very ideah of chasing yo' outa yo' own home! It makes me want to reach for my daddy's ole hunting rifle…"

"There's someone coming," I interrupted her. "I must go. Love to all."

I hung up quickly and did a little jig round the kitchen. There wasn't anyone coming, but I didn't want her to start thinking of questions and I calculated that a dramatic ending would get things moving.

You see, Mum has custody of me, but Dad's not too happy about all these stepfathers and has a firm of solicitors keep an eye on things. They cross-examine Mum – in a very civilized way – before they hand over each dollop of alimony, and when I was a kid Dad had one or two goes at getting custody, or pretended to. I reckon that was just to make sure Mum looked after me. Thanks, Dad. Now that I'm old and cynical, I see how I can make use of it.

My elation at my brilliance lasted all of two minutes, then my seesaw dipped and I started to feel depressed again. What I needed was a counter-weight on the other end to keep me permanently up. Jakes I to III chained to it and their end in molten lava ought to do the trick.

Anyway, without warning, I felt the way I had last night in my hallucination. The whole world was rotten and I was sick of it. All the greed and starvation and pollution and stupidity and the way we lived: the whole set up seemed to be crushing me. The entire world stank. I didn't want any part of it. I could have cried I felt so helpless and miserable. No, that's not true. If I'm going to be honest, I have to admit I did cry. I felt so alone and different to everyone else and as though I didn't belong anywhere, and I didn't want to because there wasn't anywhere worth belonging, and I was worthless anyway.

My tears splashed onto the kitchen table. I was quite moved by this. It somehow seemed to prove that my feelings were genuine. This wasn't self-indulgence. I was a truly tragic figure.

I'd like to make it clear that I don't normally go about crying, even if I feel like it. I did believe those things, though. Some of the time, anyway. Well, put it like this: I did when I wasn't thinking about sex.

I made myself another coffee and sat down to think things out. The mess I'd stirred up would take a while to settle and there was no guarantee I'd win. What was needed was another spoke in the wheel of Jake's used car. His prick in the spokes would be ideal. What I had to do was make it impossible for them to settle things the way they wanted before term began. Then, I hoped, it would be too late to transfer me to Borstal College.

I had another brain-wave. What I had to do was disappear. They'd be so preoccupied with attempting to explain that away to Dad's legal vultures, they'd never dare go ahead with plans to get rid of me. I could already hear the lawyers purring to Mum, "If we could just clarify what you're saying, madam." (That's legal-speak for, "Who d'you think you're trying to fool, you gold-digging little tramp?") "You claim you are heartbroken by Michael's absence, yet you are trying to get shot of him permanently. Is that correct, Mrs Shyster?"

Yes, a disappearing act would definitely swing it.

But where to? It was still two months to term. I could stay with a succession of friends, but it would be too easy to find me. If I had a fishing boat, I could live off the fruits of the sea. Don't dream, I told myself, think of something. Until then, I hadn't realized how difficult it was to disappear for two months.

First thing, wherever I went, I needed money. There immediately sprang to mind the nauseating vision of Jake carelessly slinging a wad of notes into the drawer of the mandatory antique dresser, after making sure that Mum was watching. Naturally. I went and fetched it. The notes were rolled up with an elastic band round them. All part of the image. Tax-free spending money. Untraceable, unlike plastic. I flattened them out. Tens, twenties and fifties. I didn't bother to count them. There was obviously enough to live on for two months.

But what to do precisely? I needed to lose myself so that no one could find me, and to go somewhere where my hallucinations wouldn't get me arrested. A padded cell on a radioactive island sounded ideal.

If I could find some way to get out of this modern world, that would be perfect. It would give me time to get my hallucinations under control and balance the seesaw. What I wanted was a purer, simpler lifestyle.

Suddenly, I had another brain-wave. I was definitely firing on all cylinders, like a vintage used car. I remembered an advert I'd seen. Something like *Escape from Today*. It was for holidays in horse-drawn caravans. In the state of mind I was in then, that seemed like the perfect solution. I got the local paper out of the bin and after going through it twice found the ad. There was a picture of a smiling family, a smiling horse and smiling proprietors. The latter were so far from the truth they could have been prosecuted by the Advertising Standards people, as you'll see.

I finished my breakfast in a much more cheerful frame of mind and crept upstairs to pack my rucksack. It suddenly occurred to me that I was leaving the way clear for Jake to screw as noisily as he wanted. So I went back down to the bathroom and found Mum's sponge bag. There was a back compartment with a zip where she kept her spare cards of pills. I'd found them while snibbing round one day. There was only one packet left in the chemist's envelope, and I seemed to remember there'd been three before. It was an easy sort of mistake, I reckoned, to think you'd got a spare packet left when in fact you'd started on your last one. I pocketed the packet. That would put paid to Jake's Bronco Bill act for one night at least, and sow some disharmony as well. That was definitely a spoke in his used hot-rod.

I looked round to see what else I could do.

Jake's car keys were on a table by the sofa. Where he'd tossed them no doubt. He was always casually tossing things about the place. It was part of the who-cares-about-possessions image. The answer was, he did. Status symbols were the only things which convinced him he existed. Part of the status came from pretending they were not important.

Once I'd said, "I want to learn to drive." I was miles too young, of course.

He tossed the car keys to me. Real low, so I had to grovel to catch them. "Go, teach yourself," he said, looking at Mum for her to exclaim at his virile directness.

"Oh, Jake," she squealed obligingly. "Don't be silly. He doesn't know how."

"Best way to learn is to experiment, Doris."

"It's dangerous. He hasn't got a licence."

"He can play with the gears and back up and down the drive. OK, Mike?"

"OK, Jake," I mimicked him.

"Be careful," Mum begged.

I ground the gears a couple of times and Jake soon appeared in the doorway. He shouted something and I scraped the car against a wall.

"Look what you're bloody doing!" he yelled. "Are you blind?" He ran down the drive. "What's the matter with you? Can't you use a steering wheel?"

"I'm learning," I said innocently.

"D'you know how much a respray costs?"

He told me the answer for several weeks.

I tossed his keys down the back of the sofa. He'd have had a few drinks and wouldn't be certain that he'd left them on the table. That would get their day going with Jake in a vile mood.

I felt quite pleased with myself. I noted that I seemed to be even more prone to mood swings than usual. But that wasn't really surprising. Thanks to Karen, I'd had more stuff than usual. Whoops – what a giveaway! Hush yo' mouth, honey chile. Oh, well, I said I'd be honest. Mum needed The Cottage to unwind, and once in a while, I needed to get outside myself (that's a pun on ecstasy) to get through the stress of exams.

You're probably thinking that I was a bit over-confident, still expecting Mum to want to keep me in the happy home given my track record and this morning's antics. You'd think she'd be glad to get rid of me. But what you've got to remember is Mum's image of herself.

She is the attractive young widow, battling against the world to give her talented son a good start in life. Never mind that she's divorced not widowed, not so young (though still fairly attractive, I have to admit) and that the only sacrifices she makes are to maintain the image itself. This is all effortlessly overlooked. The image is what she lives for. Take my word for it. We lawyers are keen observers of human motivation.

Whistling happily I closed the door of Lobster Pot Cottage behind me. The two plump specimens I'd caught were not even aware of the trap they were in. I set out feeling pretty cocksure, being at that time, of course, ignorant of what the future held.

ESCAPE FROM TODAY

I skipped downhill to the jetty. It was a fresh, clear morning. A strong smell of seaweed and sewage braced the early morning walkers who all seemed to be clutching newspapers like security blankets. A few polystyrene chip trays were being bounced against the stones of the jetty by the tide.

I took Mum's pills and slung them out towards the Isle of Wight, which was fourteen miles distant. They rose on a breeze, a seagull swooped and they were borne out of sight. Well, not quite. That's what I wanted to happen. What they did was flutter down onto the waves about a condom's length from the jetty. I watched them float backwards and forwards making friends with the chip trays.

I started to wonder who would find them. Perhaps when the tide ebbed they'd be carried out to sea and picked up by the lifeboat, like a message in a bottle. "What's it mean, skipper?" "It's from someone in difficulty, lad." "How can you tell, skipper?" "Marriage on the rocks."

I must have thought that was quite funny, because I suddenly realized I was leaning over the parapet giggling and two kids with fishing nets were staring at me. They looked as though they'd sneaked out of some self-catering holiday home and left their parents to sleep off the hangover they'd got at the club last night.

"You're too young to understand," I told them, and picked up my rucksack. When I looked back they were using their nets to try to fish out the card with the pretty plastic bubbles.

I set out to walk to the horse caravan place. As far as I could guess, it was about three miles. I could have taken a taxi but I didn't want to leave more clues than necessary.

The area I was heading for was called Steeple Heath. It was a sandy plateau and all that grew there were pine trees, heather, gorse and rhododendron bushes. When I was a kid I used to cycle about the heath and the animal tracks I followed seemed to go on for ever. Away from the few roads which skirted it there were black pools of still water surrounded by quicksand. The plateau was punctured by wild valleys which had once been farmed, but for some reason they'd been abandoned and become jungles. There were a few houses in some of the valleys, but the people were odd and didn't welcome strangers snooping about. Locally, it was said that Heath only married Heath.

The area teemed with rabbits, foxes, badgers and different species of deer. When I wasn't imagining being a lobster fisherman, I imagined being a hunter, dressing in skins and living off the land. I planned to build myself a hut and saw myself eventually being accepted by the other Heath dwellers.

I was well into the Heath when I suddenly felt I was being watched. I tried to look round without turning my head. In a clump of trees, I saw a horse standing half-concealed watching me. A white, barkless branch curved upwards near its head and at first sight I thought the animal was a unicorn. When I held my hand out to it, it fled as though it knew it should not be seen. I wanted it to be a unicorn because if it was, the Heath would really be the mythical place where my dreams could come true.

I must have been walking for about two hours, when I found a sign which told me something useful. I turned off down a narrow road. The pine trees on each side all seemed to be oozing sap so there was a strong sweet smell in the undisturbed air. Waxy grass grew out of the dust and encroached on the tarmac. I was hot from carrying my rucksack, my legs were tired, even though it was not really that far, and my feet felt as though they'd somehow shrunk inside my shoes.

The nearer I got to the stables, the less confident I felt. Would they just let me drive off in one of their contraptions? I could imagine some old bastard cross-examining me and amusing himself by trying to humiliate me with comments about my age, like in The Jolly Sailor.

After about another ten miles, the road ended at a wide farm gate with a notice-board nailed on it. There was garish lettering which said, AWAY FROM TODAY HOLIDAYS. Under that, a brochure was crucified behind a sheet of polythene. It showed the different types of caravan available, the route you had to follow and where campsites had been arranged. There wasn't much freedom of the open road about it.

It promised that on at least one night of your holiday there would be a surprise visit by someone from the stables who would turn up at your campsite to entertain you with folk songs round the campfire. And no doubt make a surprise check on how you were treating their property.

I took note of the route and went through the gate. This time I had to walk about half a mile before I came to a farmhouse and stables, all as neat as a children's picture book. I sat down in the trees to cool off and psyche myself up before going in for the kill. When I felt calm I brushed off the dust, combed my hair and thought myself into the right frame of mind for dealing with supercilious adults.

The farmhouse was built of red bricks, smaller than modern ones, and had a thatched roof which was covered in green, olde worlde chicken wire. One door said OFFICE so I went in. It looked as though it had once been a storeroom. There was a long counter across the far end, rough floorboards and rafters instead of a ceiling. Over all the walls were paintings of caravans and horses which made you wish the artist had been given a camera as a child. In between the pictures were strips of leather studded with horse brasses. I can never see what use they are except for flagellation.

There was no one there so I shuffled about until I discovered a creaky floorboard, then rocked backwards and forwards. That made a door behind the counter open pretty quickly and I glimpsed through it a big fitted kitchen with microwave, deep freeze, Aga cooker: like us, they'd really got away from today.

A girl about twelve years old came in. She'd got brand new pointy breasts sticking through her T-shirt and I could imagine her begging to be allowed to wear a bra, and her mother saying what for, you'll have to soon enough, and all the usual stuff. She had tight jeans and her hair was pulled back in a ponytail so that she looked as though she worked with horses or was a ballet dancer. She was obviously one of those girls who loved herself.

"Good morning," she said. "Can I help you?"

It sounded as though she'd learnt that by heart and really wished you'd drop dead.

"Hallo," I said, smiling affably to put her at her ease. "I'd like to hire a caravan."

"They're all booked."

That had not occurred to me.

"I only want a small one," I went on, "and I'd

even settle for a pony instead of a horse." I don't know why I put on that tone. It would only get her back up.

"Ponies don't pull vans," she told me contemptuously. She gave a sulky wiggle of her shoulders and switched on the computer on a ledge behind the counter. When it was loaded she clicked on something and looked pleased. "There aren't any vacancies," she enjoyed telling me. "You have to book in advance."

I took a tougher line. "Can I see whoever runs this place, please?"

She shrugged again and went away.

Through the window I could see her strolling across the yard to a row of stables about five minutes away. She wasn't hurrying.

I leaned over the counter and turned the screen round. The page showed today's date and a list of names against two or four berth vans. I decided that since they were all booked I'd better be someone who had booked one. Two berth would do me, not being greedy.

One name caught my eye. Mrs Pikkarse, I swear it. I couldn't resist that so I clicked on the name to see what would happen. All her details came up on screen: name, address, dates, deposit, balance to pay, booking number, instructions for finding this place, insurance details. Why would they want all that on their screen, I wondered, unless it was a standard page they printed out and sent to each customer.

Next to the computer sat a printer. I pushed the ON button experimentally. It came on. I clicked on FILE and PRINT PAGE. A booking confirmation form for Mrs Pikkarse spewed out of the printer. I removed it, switched off the printer and put the screen back to the list of names.

I read the address and details carefully, then folded the sheet up and bent it a few times for verisimilitude. I'd noticed a pile of envelopes on the shelf so I took one, crumpled that up as well and put Jake's money and the form in it. Then I put it in my pocket, the one with a zip, as I thought that looked more convincing.

I had another glance through the window. Miss Ponytail was just coming out of the stables. She was following a woman in baggy khaki trousers and an orange smock top. The woman strode along like someone who felt she was surrounded by fools. Ponytail had to trot to keep up.

I did a little tap dance down to the other end of the room and made a great display of studying the pictures.

The woman came in and snapped, "Morning," at me. Her subtext read: direct, no nonsense, masterful with animals, sees no reason to treat people differently. "What seems to be the trouble?" She made it clear she thought I was mentally retarded.

I marched smartly up to the counter.

"Good morning," I said, politely thrusting out my hand in my best respectful-younger-generation style. I made my handshake firm. "I've come to collect a two-berth caravan." I was gambling on a twelve-year-old kid not having much clout round this place.

"What name?" the old mare snorted.

"Pikk-ar-sé," I said, making it sound foreign. "My mother booked in April and sent a seventy pound deposit," I recited, trying to sound eager to be helpful.

"Ah, yes," she grunted, clicking on the name and bringing the details up on screen. "Where-abouts you from?" she asked, making it casual but obviously checking.

No fool, I told myself. So watch it.

I named the town, then the street and lastly, as an afterthought, the house number, being as help-ful as I could. A nice, hesitant-boy image.

"It's all here, Davinia," she told Ponytail.

Davinia! It was too good to be true.

I leapt gallantly to her defence. "I'm afraid I may have confused the young lady," I apologized.

"He didn't say," she started to explain, but was swept aside.

"Davinia's always got her head in the clouds," the old mare informed me, teaching Ponytail never to stand too near a beast of vicious disposition because you're likely to get kicked in the gut.

"She was trying to be helpful," I insisted compas-sionately. I was so innocuous I made myself want to puke. I could have been a *Blue Peter* presenter.

Ponytail looked as though she'd like to see the

knacker's men go to work on me. I leered at her breasts to keep her quiet. If only she knew the revenge she was going to have on the old mare when the real Mrs Pikkarse turned up, she'd have offered me a quick ride bareback.

"It's for you and your mother, is it?" the old mare demanded, wanting to get everything tied up neatly.

"Yes. There's just Mother and me. Dad…" I let the explanation tail away. "People always think it must be for a married couple when Mother books something."

"Mrs Pikkarse not here?"

"No. That's why I'm so early. I want to get to Stowham by lunch-time. That's where we're going to meet and have a meal. Mum's coming down by train and that's the nearest point to the station on the route in your brochure." (Subtext: we will adhere religiously to your rules.)

"Have you got the booking confirmation?"

I fumbled with my zip pocket, pulled out the envelope and offered her the form.

"There's still the balance to pay. Then we'll give you some instruction in handling."

I counted off five of Jake's fifties inside the envelope as though I was nervous at having so much money in my possession.

"Now all you have to do is sign this form to say you will keep to the route on the map we give you. It's for insurance purposes."

She shoved a form in front of me. I plucked the

name Adrian out of the last twelve hours and signed it Adrian Pikkarse.

After this we went over to the stables. Davinia dragged a reluctant brown and white horse out of its stall while her mother announced that she'd get the tack.

Davinia introduced us. "This is Montgomery."

"Right. Dobbin it is," I replied, running my eyes over the pointy bits of her T-shirt and her crotch-tight jeans. As soon as her mother returned, Davinia went off to sulk and I felt safer.

I was allowed to lead Dobbin round to the back of the stables, where the caravan was parked. He curled his lips at the sight of it. I knew how he felt. It was painted an eye-searing red, green and blue, with every prominent edge picked out in white. If this was what gypsy caravans had looked like, I was not surprised that they'd migrated to the chrome and net-curtained hearses they favoured nowadays. It made even those appear tasteful.

Baggy Pants gave me instructions about backing Dobbin between the shafts (without shafting him in the process), not jerking the reins, tightening the girth and allowing stacks of room when turning corners. She made me drive round the yard about fifty times. She snapped out all her orders in short sentences and seemed to think that things would go more quickly if Dobbin and I changed places. I was as humble as a leper doing a charity advert.

After about an hour I began to worry that Mrs Pikkarse might turn up. But the old mare suddenly seemed to decide that I was ineducable and snapped, "That will do. You can go." After a pause she added grudgingly, "Have a good time."

I halted Dobbin by the office, slung my rucksack through the caravan door, then lashed him into a plod which seemed to be his only speed.

We went the right way to start with, but I had another route in mind, and when we reached a crossroads we shot off, at a plod, widdershins. Stuff their insurance, I thought gladly. Were gypsies insured?

I inhaled deeply, birds sang and dappled sunlight dodged the scaly trunks and turned Dobbin into a lithe mythological creature. I've escaped from today, I sighed, and allowed myself a modest sip at the chalice of success.

You'll not be surprised to hear that my euphoria was, as usual, short-lived. I found myself wondering; did I really have the nerve to do what I'd just done? The answer was no. It was The Jolly Sailor all over again. I'd not done it, my hallucination had. Or had it? Was any of this happening? After losing my clothes last night, what I needed was some sort of reality check.

I promptly had my fourth brain-wave of the day.

When I was a kid I had this problem. I'd be in bed and need a pee, but instead of waking up I'd dream that I was in the toilet or standing behind a tree or something and start to go. As soon as I felt the warmth on my thighs I'd wake up. I was so humiliated I never told anyone, instead I invented this arm-swinging reality test. Whenever I went to the lavatory, to check that I was really there and not lying in bed, I'd swing my arms madly so that I'd be bound to feel the duvet and wake up. You'd think I'd start dreaming the swinging or not think about it at all in the dream, but it always worked and from then on I woke up.

I didn't see why this shouldn't work in a hallucination as well. So I shouted, "I'm hallucinating!" and swung my arms. I nearly broke my wrist on the edge of the caravan. I leaned forward and felt the texture of Dobbin's tail. I was awake all right.

In a way this was more worrying than if everything *had* been a hallucination. What I'd feared, and what the treacherous part of me had wanted, had happened: my hallucinations had taken over.

I shrugged. What did it matter? I wanted to get away, didn't I, and I was doing so more effectively than if it had been left to my normal self. I decided to stop worrying. There was nothing I could do about it and I didn't care – because in order to care, something had to be important to you and nothing was.

"Gee up, Dobbin," I said.

He plodded along without any trouble. I got the impression that he did not have much imagination. I thought about renaming him Jake, but I'm against cruelty to animals, fox hunting and meat-eating (except at mealtimes).

That was a hollow joke against myself, but it led me to reflect on my lack of moral fibre. There didn't seem to be any principle I would not abandon if it was expedient. Just offer me sex or food and I was putty.

I imagined being propositioned by a Slav with a fur-collared coat.

"We want you to betray your country."

"Never! It's a matter of principle."

"Have you met Miss Kinksky, your nymphomaniac contact?"

"Could you give me more information about what you have in mind?"

"Here are free tickets for an ox roast."

"I was feeling peckish."

I clucked cheerfully at Dobbin. My seesaw was up again.

We clip-clopped slowly away from the specified route. By the time they missed us we'd be lost in the maze of tracks which criss-crossed the heath, or sunk in a stagnant pool, or impaled on a unicorn's horn.

I'd escaped from today all right, and probably from tomorrow as well, given my mental state.

ON THE ROAD

The caravan's roof was made of maintenance-free fibreglass. Really eco-friendly. Inside there was one room which, apart from the rounded ceiling, was just like a modern caravan: bunks, cooker, fridge, with a cubicle in one corner where you could shit and shower at the same time.

I sat on the doorstep, wedged my shoulder in the corner of the porch-like bit and held the reins loosely while letting Dobbin do the steering. The ride was quite smooth as the caravan had pneumatic tyres.

Behind his blinkers, Dobbin had tunnel vision and he didn't even flinch when a tractor roared past us. That was the only vehicle we encountered on our way to Lower Steeple, which was objective number one. I knew the village from my biking days. All I remembered seeing there was a general store, a pub, a church and about one house. What I planned to do, before emulating the Flying

Dutchman and disappearing into the mists of time, was stock up with plenty of provisions.

I knew that the road beyond the village was a dead-end. People drove down there to a grassy picnic area but that was as far as most of them got. The Heath wasn't tourist pretty. It was a monotonous peninsula of land which led nowhere.

I reckoned that once I was lost in there they'd have to get the air-sea rescue helicopter out to find me among all the pines and little valleys. I couldn't see them bothering. What would Ponytail's mater be able to tell the police?

"Constable, I want to report a stolen horse and caravan."

"Do you have any idea who might have taken them, madam?"

"A young man calling himself Adrian Pikkarse."

"You're sure of the name, madam?"

"Of course I'm sure, Constable. He signed the insurance form."

"The insurance form?"

"When anyone hires one of my vans they have to sign an insurance agreement."

"Hire, madam?"

"Yes. He gave me two hundred and fifty pounds and took my horse and caravan."

"You hired it to him?"

"Yes, but it was for someone else. Are you going on with these fool questions all day, Constable, or are you going out to catch the little blighter?"

"I understood you to say it was stolen."

"It was, as good as. It wasn't supposed to be hired to him. He deceived my daughter. I've got the real Pikkarses up at my place now. What are you going to do about it?"

"It's not our job to sort out your double bookings, madam."

I was just enjoying imagining this conversation and the triumph of Ponytail when she reminded Mumsy that she'd said there was no caravan booked for me, when a voice from up ahead broke through my daydreaming.

"Hey, tinker. 'Ave 'ee any gelding irons?"

Three peasant youths were sitting on a fence. Dobbin stopped politely. I tried to flick the reins inconspicuously, but he recognized a good excuse for a break when one fell in his path.

"Morning," I said, dead matey and casual, while my pulse revved up to about twice its usual rate.

"How be 'ee, tinker?" one of them asked.

"Come far this morning?" another wanted to know.

"Thy beast be ready to rest," the third observed.

The trio were grinning sadistically. They were in control and my caravan anchored me to the spot. What is it about me that attracts these types? It was The Jolly Sailor all over again.

"Nice day for sitting on a fence," I retorted.

"Sharp as a knife, this 'un," number two said.

"Hey, tinker," number one began again, "can 'ee sell I a pair o' gelding irons?"

"What?"

"'Ee got an old boar at home needs castrating."

"'Ee means his stepdad."

Numbers two and three almost fell off the fence laughing.

"I'm not a tinker," I explained unnecessarily, and fatally wounded myself.

"Well, I coulda swore 'ee were," number one said, gaping in amazement.

"'Ee do look like a tinker up there, doan 'ee?" number three echoed him.

"Sorry I can't help you," I said weakly and flicked the reins.

"Where be 'ee a-goin'?" number two asked.

"To knackers, by look o' yon beast," number one remarked, which threw them into hysterics again.

Suddenly they seemed to grow bored. Judging by the dimensions of their foreheads I surmised that their concentration span was about the same as an educationally challenged goldfish.

"'Ere, let I help thee," number three offered.

He leaned forward and gave Dobbin a cut across his rump with a stick he'd been chewing. Dobbin gave a whinny and leapt forward. I was thrown back through the door of the caravan.

"Degenerate bloody yokels," I yelled uselessly. They were so inbred they were genetically modified. Even their dialect was about a century out of date.

We began to descend the hill into the village, gathering pace with every stride. Luckily, I didn't let go of the reins. I scrambled up and as the hill got steeper I hauled at Dobbin and kept giving the van a bit of brake to slow it down. I could visualize it sweeping over Dobbin and crushing him before hurtling over a precipice and taking a short cut to the bottom of the valley.

After about thirty seconds Dobbin seemed ready to resume his normal pace, if he could. I hung on to the brake, hauled on the reins and gradually we slowed down.

I swore until the adrenaline drained from my system, then I tried to salvage my self-respect by telling myself that the peasants had had a bit of fun at my expense, but they'd also done me a favour. I'd been pretending I was escaping from the present but they'd shown me it took only one glance at my garish caravan to see that I was a holiday-maker playing at gypsies.

We trundled into the village with me feeling a bit depressed as I'd not really done anything to satisfy my feeling of disgust at today's world. It suddenly seemed urgent that I remedy that.

Dobbin stopped outside the village shop without being told to and looked over his shoulder at me with a self-satisfied smirk.

"Good dog," I said, to put him in his place.

The shop was an ordinary house with an old wooden notice nailed over the front window. There was curling lino on the floor, an open fire-place and a table for a counter. The shelves were planks balanced on piles of bricks. Behind the table stood a frail old lady who smiled at me understandingly when I went in. I was so moved by her compassion that I bought the place up.

I spent seventy quid on food and cider and anything I fancied. It took me three journeys to carry all the goodies out. The old bird just stood there with her thinning hair pulled back in a bun, and nodded as if giving me her blessing.

In one corner I noticed a stack of aerosol cans. The labels said they were quick-drying spray-paint, the sort you use to touch up cars when you've scraped them on a wall in the drive. God knows why she stocked them. Probably some smart salesman who'd lost his way had palmed them off on her. The sight of them, plus my recent humiliation, led to an idea forming in my ever-fertile brain.

The cans were marked at one-twenty each and there must have been forty or fifty of them. I returned after my last journey to examine them. Judging by the dust, they'd been there since the internal combustion engine was invented. Apart from one red, the only colours left were dull browns and olive green; shades car manufacturers shun.

"How much do you want for those spray paints?" I asked, pointing at them.

"They're one-twenty each," she said, pursing her lips. "Dreadful expensive for what they are, in my opinion."

"Not much demand for them," I suggested. I

doubted that the peasants would have got as far, educationally, as graffiti.

"Sold two for the carnival, as I recall."

"I'll give you fifteen quid for the lot."

"Twenty," she snapped, still smiling sweetly. With her thinning hair she suddenly reminded me of those vultures which shove their heads into carcasses up to their shoulders.

"It's a deal."

"Take the box," she invited generously.

I staggered out with my rattling cargo. I felt content that ninety quid of Jake's money had gone to such a nice little old lady. I hoped the peasants wouldn't mug her. They'd probably come off worse if they tried.

Feeling more cheerful, I shoved the box inside the caravan door with the rest of the things.

"Wagons roll," I instructed Dobbin, and lashed him with a spare length of rein. He put his head down and heaved. I let him strain for a few seconds, then took the brake off.

I glanced back at the shop. The old lady had emerged from behind her table and was standing in the shadow of the doorway.

She had turkey legs and claws instead of feet.

I thrashed about a bit, banging my arms on the caravan woodwork, but it wasn't a dream. Nothing was what it seemed. By this time I'd forgotten about Karen's pills and Anna's worries. I just thought everything was a con; the whole world pretended to be one thing, but it was all hypocrisy. Beneath the smiling exterior was pollution and disease.

My seesaw had dipped just when I wasn't expecting it.

What was happening to me? Was I becoming schizoid? I'd been thinking of the little old lady as a bird, and the next thing I knew she'd been transformed into one. It wouldn't be long at this rate before I started stabbing people because I thought they were aliens trying to invade my body. I definitely needed to get lost until I was straightened out.

I was distracted from further thought about my mental state because at that moment we were passing what appeared to be the village's one and only house. Outside it was parked a painter's van and on its rear door was an immaculate advert. My one can of red paint was the same colour as the lettering on the ad. I remembered my desire to demonstrate my disgust at today's world. I jumped down leaving Dobbin to plod on alone.

There was no one in sight so I gave a concentrated burst of spray to each of the letters and to a picture of a paint pot. That left blobby runs of quick-drying paint bleeding out of an announcement about the high standard of workmanship guaranteed. Then I doubled back up the road to catch Dobbin.

The van probably belonged to some sad little guy who'd worked hard for years to build up his business and be able to afford a smart new vehicle. I knew that. But I wanted to do something to show

how I felt about the dull, plodding Dobbins of the world who are wrapped up in their own petty affairs. All they want to do is make you into one of them.

That doesn't mean to say I was proud of what I'd done. Half of me wasn't. But I felt I had to do it to break my brainwashing. What I'd done was a gob in the face of the world. If you can't understand that, you might as well stop reading now.

I came to the end of the tarmacked road and bounced across a deserted picnic area. Ahead of me the real Heath began. I chose a track that looked as though it led to the most remote part.

As the morning passed I switched tracks several times while keeping to the same general direction. I wanted to make it impossible for the old mare from the holiday firm to find me, even if she set out on horseback in pursuit.

By about four o'clock I reckoned I was pretty safe and Dobbin, not being used to cross-country treks, was knackered, so I started to look for somewhere to camp. I found a site screened by a clump of trees. There was a stream nearby and when I'd tanked Dobbin up I tethered him in the centre of a patch of lush grass. He gave a snort which sounded like: "Hay?"

"Grass," I told him. "All this processed food is bad for you." He munched without much show of appreciation while I set to work.

I couldn't be a gypsy but at least I could be less conspicuous. From the air I'd stand out like a distress flare. I clambered up on top of my caravan with an armful of spray cans. I just pressed the button on each one until it was empty, then jettisoned it. I worked my way along the roof making wavy brown and green stripes. Then I did the same along the sides until I had a unique, camouflaged caravan. I sprayed the spokes alternately brown and green and did slashes on the tyres in the hope that they'd blur as the wheels went round or go backwards if ever I was filmed.

When I finished I felt quite euphoric. The old mare would have a two-headed foal if she could see her precious bloody van. I wasn't sure where I was going next day, but even if I was picked up by the police (unlikely) I'd probably done enough so that Jake and Mum wouldn't dare pack me off to their private borstal. By now Dad and Lois should have got their legal piranhas on to them.

Somehow the pear-drop smell of the paint had got into the van and by the time I'd had a snack I was feeling woozy. When I looked out of the door the trees were swaying backwards and forward. I blinked, but that made no difference.

"I'm going for a walk," I told Dobbin. "I'm inadvertently high from sniffing spray cans."

Dobbin lifted his tail and expressed his opinion.

I set off, following the stream through the trees. I staggered a bit because the ground kept moving. When the trees finally ended I thought I'd stumbled across the caravan equivalent of an elephants' graveyard.

I'd come out on a low headland and between me and the sea were semicircular humps like the roofs of giant caravans. Had they roamed the Heath in antediluvian times? I wondered. They seemed to have lost their wheels and sunk into the ground. But the bizarre thing about them which made my stomach churn in panic was that they were all camouflaged in the same way as my van.

What the humps turned out to be were disused army huts from the Second World War. You see them sometimes being used by farmers as barns, but this place was so isolated that they'd been left to rot down for archeologists.

I wandered between the huts until I reached the edge of the land and was looking out over grey, heaving waves. The sun had gone and sand-dunes descended like black steps to sea level. In the distance an automated lighthouse signalled to me like a drowning hand. There was not a craft in sight. The world was empty and had been drained of colour. It was how I wanted it.

The stream I had been following joined another one to make a mini river. It was so sluggish that it scarcely dented the waves where it flowed into the sea. About every five minutes there was a sudden surge of reddish water. It reminded me of the Nile. I've never seen the Nile, I don't mean that, but apparently at a certain time every year there's a flood and the water changes colour. The ancient Egyptians used to think it was one of their gods, Osiris or someone, dying, and he was supposed to come back to life later in the year when his sister, Isis, collected the pieces of his dismembered body. More myths. I guessed that probably what it was with my Nile was some factory upstream discharging pollution into it.

After I'd watched this for a bit I decided to commit suicide. It wasn't Jake and Mum or anything. I didn't even think of them then. It was just that there didn't seem any point in going on.

You needn't think I was doing the cry for help routine or any of that Samaritan shit. For one thing there was no one around to hear me, and for another if people want to commit suicide, let them get on with it without interfering, I say.

Once we had this guy from the Samaritans come to speak to us at school to tell us what a great job they were doing. He went on about the value of each individual life and how they were forcing people who were undecided to go on living. We were all bored out of our skulls and trying to stop giggling. When it was question time my mate Theo got up, holding his notebook and screwing up his face in a fascinated expression, and asked, "Are you in favour of capital punishment?"

The Samaritan got as far as saying, "I see what you're driving at. That's a very good question." When Theo suddenly leapt up again and said, "Sorry. That question was for last week's speaker. This is the one I was told to ask you." We all killed ourselves laughing, and the Samaritan didn't look as though he wanted to save anyone.

All I'm telling you that for is to show that I didn't have even a silent fart of an idea of being saved.

I climbed down to the beach next to where the river flowed into the sea. I reckoned there should be treacherous currents about there just waiting to sweep me away. I got undressed and waded out up to my chin but I was still not drowning and I couldn't find a current anywhere.

I went deeper and started to swim. If you can swim, you can't stop yourself. I tried, but I just floated and got cold. My whole life was a farce. I couldn't even commit suicide properly.

I realized that getting rid of my clothes had been a bad move. I should have done a Virginia Woolf: filled my pockets with stones and tried to walk out to the lighthouse.

I decided I'd have to wait until I got tired and sank. I thought I might be able to hurry things up by swimming upriver against the current. That ought to be more tiring. So I struck out for the river mouth. This seemed to be working, as by the time I made it to the river my arms were beginning to ache.

Behind me the lighthouse flashed in time with my strokes and its beam turned the banks flesh-pink so that I imagined I was swimming between giant thighs. Then there was a surge of reddish water, like the giant was giving birth, and I began to laugh.

Once I started I couldn't stop. I shrieked so

uncontrollably I was in danger of drowning. There was I in this bloody flux between gargantuan thighs, trying to end my life by swimming back to an existence before I was born because that was the last time I'd really belonged anywhere and been happy.

I stopped swimming and lay there screaming with laughter. I didn't drown because after the surge the river level fell and it was too shallow. I rolled out onto the bank, covered in red mud, gasping for air as though I'd just been born.

All I can remember is lying there laughing and screaming hysterically. Once again I ended the day naked, but I didn't care. I was dying of laughter. I drew great whoops of breath and the laughter went on and on manically. Eventually everything went blank and that was the end of my suicide attempt.

THE GREEN MAN

When I woke up there was a pre-dawn light seeping out of the waves which were lapping on the wet sand near my head. The lighthouse was still winking but it seemed to have receded to the horizon. I was cold and felt woozier than when I'd made the evolutionary leap onto the shore the previous night. I seemed to be making a habit of sleeping rough, but my feverish state suggested I wasn't cut out for this sort of life.

I bundled up my clothes and hauled myself up the dunes. The stream led me back to the caravan. I had a shower because I was such a mess and I lit all the burners on the gas cooker to warm myself up but I still shivered uncontrollably the whole time. Even soup for breakfast didn't make me feel any better and I kept getting alternate spasms of shivering and sweating. It hadn't occurred to me that I might get ill. I felt so low I even thought about going home, but if I did that, then I'd be dead. The real me – whoever that was – would be. In a different way to what I was aiming for last night.

I decided to push on and try to throw off whatever it was I'd caught. I put on my cagoule and went to wake up Dobbin. Do horses sleep? I never saw him with his eyes closed. He was smirking as usual, sort of saying, You can't take it, hey?

"A nice tight girth for you today, my four-legged lackey," I told him through chattering teeth. "Just to show you who's in charge." He drew breath at the vital moment and to my feverish vision he seemed to inflate like a hot air balloon. I didn't feel up to a tussle so I let him win.

We plodded off, leaving the aerosol cans behind. The scenery passed at a distance, unreal and insubstantial. My head throbbed and laser lights played behind my eyes.

This was when things started to get odd. But really. If you thought my hallucinations had been in overdrive – OD for short – for some time, all I can say is, you ain't seen nuthin' yet. The final proof that I'd gone over the top was that I didn't think things were all that odd at the time. Occasionally, I had half an idea that not everything was kosher, but I was able to shrug it off.

I sat and let Dobbin go where he wanted. He took me deeper into the Heath than I'd ever been before. I felt that this was primal land, how the world had been before time began. I was going back to an era of purity where I was meant to be.

The scattered clumps of trees and scrub gave way to denser growth. Trees arched overhead, making a tunnel, and the light flickering through the leaves made it impossible to focus my eyes even when my thoughts were coherent.

I had no idea where we were. I'd heard of people getting lost on the Heath. I wasn't bothered about that, as long as I stayed lost. The only thing I worried about was blundering out onto a road into the waiting arms of Mum and Jake. But that didn't seem likely. There weren't even any distant traffic sounds.

Dobbin came to a halt eventually and at first I couldn't see why. Then I managed to focus on this signpost. It was plain wood with the name carved in curly old letters. All it said was ENDE.

That was appropriate, I thought. I'd reached the end of my journey. I'd found my place to escape to.

"OK," I said to Dobbin. He looked over his shoulder and smirked at me, as if he knew something I didn't. Then he plodded on.

The caravan pushed through trees, and leaves slapped against my face. Suddenly they parted and we found ourselves high up on the side of a more perfect valley than any calendar had ever offered as solace to the sad punters who tick off the days to oblivion.

All round the rim was a fortification of dense woods, while below, the valley floor was a herringbone pattern made by oddly narrow fields of different colours. In a loose circle round the bottom of the valley was a necklace of thatched houses. The thread which held them together was a road of hard-packed earth. Strangely, there was no church, but all was peaceful in the morning sun. I knew this was the place I had been drawn to. I had always felt that such a valley existed, if only I could find it.

A track sloped across the side of the valley, descending gently enough for a caravan to negotiate. As my destination neared, the fever closed in again, but I let it come, because now I could allow myself to be weak. I did not have to fight this world. By the time we reached the valley floor I could hardly sit upright. Dobbin plodded along the village street. If there were people about, I didn't see them.

I needed somewhere to rest. Telepathically, Dobbin halted outside the village inn. It was called The Green Man and the sign showed a dancing simpleton dressed in ragged green clothes. He had a turnip for a head with fruit for features, runner-bean fingers and corn sheaves for legs. He was holding a sickle and leaning over to cut his own legs from the ground.

I climbed down to the hard-packed earth of the road and stretched out my hand towards the rough wood of the inn door to support myself. It wasn't locked, and swung open as I touched it. I staggered into a large room which was an entrance hall and a bar. The space behind the bar was far wider than normal, as if commercial calculations did not apply. There were pottery beakers instead of glasses on a shelf and in place of pressure pumps there was a row of barrels on cradles with wooden taps for drawing the ale.

Across the ceiling were beams which in my feverish state seemed to breathe like exposed ribs. At one end of the room was a broad staircase of blackened wood. The whitewashed walls were decorated with images of sheaves and moons and corn dollies made of woven straw. The place seemed deserted, but no sooner had I wondered whether there was a bell somewhere, than a door behind the counter opened and a plump middle-aged woman came bustling in.

"There ye are," she said as though she'd been looking for me. "Ye'll be wanting a room, I can tell. Now I thought I'd gie 'ee the double at the end. We call it the bridal chamber on occasions, but the thing about it is ye can't hear the noise from the bar here. They do make quite a hubbub sometimes, I can tell 'ee."

She bustled about all the time, but I couldn't say exactly what she accomplished. She produced a book from behind the bar and the sort of pen you have to dip in an ink pot. "Ye just write thy name there, so Lily knows how to address thee."

I took the pen and was about to write Michael Jester when the thought formed in my fuddled brain that that might not be a good idea, so instead I started writing Adrian Pikkarse, then decided I didn't want to connect myself with the caravan place either, so, since I'd written *Ad* already, I made it into *Adam* and then put *Green* because the name of the inn was still in my head. When I'd written it, I glanced up the page at all the other signatures and for a second, in my delirium, I thought that they all said Adam Green. But the woman turned the book round briskly and I couldn't be certain.

"That's right," she said, reading and nodding approvingly. "Ye'd better call me Lily, everyone does. That or Ma. I'm not fussy." She came round the bar. "Ye just follow me and I'll show 'ee to thy chamber."

I was about to say I'd fetch my things, but she rolled on. "Doan ye worry about thy belongings. Young Jehu will bring them up directly."

At the time, I didn't find anything odd about her way of talking, which will give you some idea of how far out of it I was.

She panted up the stairs and I tagged along obediently. "Bless me," she exclaimed halfway up, "these stairs will be the death of me. Mind thy head at the top. It's a bit on the low side for a fine young fellow like 'ee."

There were more ribs across the ceiling all the way down a long corridor. "Right to the end," she said. "Journey's end, I always call it when I get there."

We passed doors in crooked frames and what with the breathing beams and my feverishness the corridor began to sway. I clutched the walls as if I was on a ship.

"Here we are," Ma Lily said at last, and I stepped through a low doorway into a room with furniture of the usual blackened wood. In the centre was a huge bed inviting me. I anchored my eyes on it to keep myself steady.

"I expect ye be wanting to rest after thy adventures, so I'll just leave 'ee as long as ye likes. When ye be ready to eat, come down and find the kitchen. There's allus something to tuck into. Ye can rely on Lily." She went away chuckling.

I flopped down onto the bed intending to take my trainers off, but as my weight subsided onto it, layer after layer of fluffed up coverings collapsed under me and I fell backwards. I drifted down and down like Alice in the rabbit hole. Through the window I could see the inn sign with the laughing raspberry mouth of the Green Man. He seemed to be falling with me, pushing me down into the earth. We were turning slowly as we fell and I put out my arms to him to stop myself. Then he clasped his bean fingers behind my back and we fell as one person.

I don't remember reaching the bottom of the hole. My last thought was that since I didn't know who I was, apart from being a sex maniac, I might as well be Adam Green or the Green Man or Icarus. Then I blacked out.

COUNTRY MATTERS

It felt like morning when I opened my eyes – the first morning after the creation of the world. I guessed that I'd slept for about twenty-four hours, and I was naked yet again.

The first thing I became aware of were mountainous pillows. I'd never seen anything like them and I was tucked between two of them like Tom Thumb. Both were the size of the bed. When I moved there was no weight in them and they rustled and gave off a scent of herbs which caressed my forehead like cool, massaging fingers. I used to know an old lady who dabbed lavender water behind her ears. I'd never seen why, but if it made her feel like this then I understood because I felt relaxed and luxurious and utterly unstressed.

There was a window at the foot of the bed, and after I'd decided I should do more with my new life than just breathe, I tried to sit up and look out. I wallowed about and discovered that I was as weak as a newborn baby, but I finally managed to prop myself up long enough to glimpse the outside world.

The first thing I saw was the inn sign. This time the Green Man's turnip face seemed to be leering at me as though he could recognize a sex maniac when he saw one. I also caught sight of a field of ripe corn. But that was all, because the effort of keeping myself upright long enough to see that much just about killed me. I let myself drop back and fell in slow motion like last night. I didn't care about being helpless because I felt great for the first time since Jake III came on the scene.

The next thing that happened was this incredible girl walked in with a breakfast tray, as though she'd been doing nothing else for years. She'd got golden hair the same colour as the corn I'd seen through the window, creamy smooth skin and a round, open, honest face with cornflower blue eyes. I'd once heard some old fart on TV raving over a girl he'd been in love with in his youth who had eyes that colour, but I'd not understood what he was on about until now. They were brighter than usual and they had the effect of making you laugh when she did, and you never wanted them to stop looking at you.

She'd got a perfect figure and all her movements were easy and fluid, like the grasses in a meadow flowing in a breeze. But the best thing about her, the most intoxicating, was her smell. I'm not kidding. She smelt somehow like the pillows: herbs and harvest and wild flowers and countryside. I know it sounds crazy, but her appearance didn't attract me even though she was gorgeous. It was her natural scent that just about drove me mad with desire.

"Ma said ye'd be ready for breakfast today," she said, as though we'd known each other for years. Her voice had a sort of laugh in it.

"I'm hungry all right," I agreed.

She put the tray down on a chest and helped me to sit up as though she knew before I started to move that I'd be weak. It was a good job that I was or I'd have done something stupid like catching hold of her, burying my face in her hair and weeping for joy. As she propped me up, the material that was stretched over her breasts brushed across my eyes like balm. I remembered Lois and her bursting blouse and wondered how I could ever have been tempted by that coarse old hag.

I've died. I'm in heaven, I thought. Then my angel began straightening the giant pillow and the scent of her body was so heavy I nearly swooned like the heroine in a nineteenth-century novel. I was immediately revived, however, because she plonked the tray down on my lap which pretty near maimed me because, in spite of my feebleness, I'd got an erection like the leaning tower of Pisa.

"Thanks," I managed to gasp. There was brown bread, honey, a flapjack type of biscuit and apple juice. A funny sort of breakfast, I thought. Perhaps this was a health food place. I tucked in ravenously, not caring.

"Is that lady I saw yesterday your mother?" I asked, to keep her there.

"Ma Lily be mother to everyone."

"She seemed to know what I wanted before I asked."

She laughed. "'Course she do. What d'ye expect? She's Ma Lily, ain't she?"

I laughed as well. I didn't get all that, but who cared. I asked: "What's your name?"

She put her head on one side. "Don't ye remember?"

My mouth full, I shook my head.

"Why, I'm Evie."

I wondered why I should remember. Perhaps I'd been told when I was delirious.

"Did you undress me?" I asked, suddenly thinking we might know each other better than I realized.

"Why, no," Evie giggled. "That were Young Jehu."

She opened the window and the breeze wafted the scent of her over me again. She leaned out and shouted to someone below, "'A be 'ere."

Perhaps the village was wondering about my camouflaged caravan, I thought, explaining away another strange remark. There seemed to be quite a few odd things here, but I put them down to the spray cans and my fever: it was me, not my surroundings, who was out of synch. With that thought, I happily dismissed the lot. Why bother? I was as comfortable as a film star and well away from where I didn't want to be.

"What's happened to my caravan?" I asked Evie's buttocks, which were covered in a patchwork skirt and just the right shape to fit into my sweaty palms. On top she wore an old-fashioned blouse with short, puffy sleeves.

She gave a wave and turned back from the window. "Oh, don't ye worry. Jus' leave everything to Young Jehu."

I shrugged contentedly. I was confident that nothing could go wrong here.

"Tell me about this village. Where am I?"

This made her laugh again. "Where be ye?" she repeated. "This be the only place. Don't ye fret. 'Tis the right place for 'ee."

"I agree," I said, looking at her meaningfully. "Move this tray, will you, and sit here so we can talk." The sex maniac felt refreshed.

She did as I said, quite simply, as though it was the normal thing to do. There was none of that silly giggling or those moronic "What have you got in mind?" sort of remarks most girls go in for.

"How long have I been here?" I asked. It had suddenly struck me that being in a fever I might have been here for more than one night. That would explain things.

"Since there were no moon."

"How long's that?"

"Why, three days, of course. Do ye remember nothin'?"

"I didn't realize. I must've been really ill then."

"Not ill, just sleeping. So I been tol'."

"Who told you?"

"Ma Lily. She do tell I everything."

"I love to hear you talk."

"Ye allus say that."

"What're you on about, Evie? I don't follow half what you say."

She just laughed, like at a secret joke. But not in a way to shut you out, which is what a lot of girls would have done. It was as if she'd never learnt all those bits of spite.

"I feel dizzy again," I said, and let myself flop down on the bed, but sideways so that my head was against her thigh.

She brushed my hair out of my eyes with her fingers.

"Shall I lie in your lap?" I asked, quoting a speech I'd learned from *Hamlet*.

"No," she said on cue.

"I mean, my head in your lap."

"Ay," she said, again on cue.

"Do you think I meant country matters?"

"I don't think nothin'." Still on cue.

"That's a fair thought to lie between a maid's legs," I went on.

"What's that?"

"Nothing."

"I must be about my duties," she said without offence, and picked up the tray.

"Did you do *Hamlet* at school?" I asked.

"School," she laughed. "Bless 'ee. I've never bin

to no school. What use be that to I?"

"Did you read it then?"

She gave a peel of laughter as if I'd said the funniest thing she'd heard that month.

"But you know *Hamlet*?" I asked in desperation.

"I never heard of 'a."

She danced out with the tray, leaving me with another puzzle to explain. If what she said was true – and I believed every word, I don't think she'd learned how to lie – that conversation we'd had about country matters was just about impossible.

I'd learned that bit of *Hamlet* because I thought calling a girl's sex "country matters" was somehow pure. It did away with all the usual words and the swearing that made use of them. It was like fresh air in a dank cellar.

I knew *Hamlet* because I'd seen a film that had made it to the local multiplex. It had got a major release because there was a big box-office star in the title role.

I had quite a bit of sympathy for Hamlet. I suppose I identified with him. He thought everything in Denmark, his country, was rotten, and I think the whole world's hypocritical and polluted. Hamlet's behaviour made sense to me. That was one of the reasons I learned the speech. The other was that I was a sex maniac.

That's not really much to do with what I'm telling you about, except that I couldn't explain how Evie knew that bit of dialogue. That was just one odd thing among a whole lot.

I suddenly thought that I might be hallucinating and reluctantly decided on a reality test. I flailed about, tentatively at first, then, as I made craters in my blissful lunar bedscape, I flung myself about with childish exuberance until I was exhausted. After that I happily ignored all the oddities of my new life, especially once I'd decided I was in love with Evie. That decision didn't take more than five minutes to reach. It was love at first scent.

I spent two days in bed getting my strength back and being waited on by Evie and Ma Lily. On the third morning, I had breakfast in bed and later got dressed and went downstairs. Sunshine seemed to come through every window and make the whole place light and fresh. I went through the door at the back of the bar into the huge kitchen as though I was at home, which I felt I was for the first time in my life.

Ma Lily was there at a vast wooden table with flour up to her elbows.

"Ah. So ye've risen at last. Just in time too."

"In time for what?"

"To taste the new bread."

There was a row of brown loaves on a side table under a window. Next to it was a blackened range which took up all the rest of the wall.

"Cut y'self a thumb," Ma Lily instructed.

"A what?" I asked dumbly.

"A thumb of bread, ye ninny."

I saw what she meant and fetched a loaf over to the big table where a carving knife lay.

"It be good bread," a voice said from behind the door.

I hadn't seen anyone there when I came in and I nearly cut my own thumb off. In a shadowy corner sat this huge, gangly guy with a head like a pumpkin. His hair stuck out round it like a halo, his ears were long and shapeless, and he had a big, loose mouth like someone had carved a hole for Hallowe'en.

"That be Young Jehu. 'A be potman," Ma Lily told me. She didn't bother to tell him who I was. Presumably he knew.

"Stay it has," Young Jehu informed me.

"Sorry?" I said, feeling foolish.

"'A means, my bread's got stay in it."

"What's that?"

"A bit extra. Give 'ee strength to keep goin' longer. That's right, bain't it, Jehu?"

"Aye, gammer. It be."

"D'ye want a piece, Jehu?" Ma Lily asked.

He shambled over to the table. I went to offer him the knife.

"'A'll use 'is own shut-knife," Ma Lily snapped abruptly.

I looked at Young Jehu then. There was something odd about him. He was lopsided and his limbs weaved about unnecessarily as he moved, but he appeared strong. He had a puzzled, good-natured expression. I realized slowly, but still with a shock, that he was not all there and so he was forbidden knives. Then I wondered why he was called Young

Jehu, when he was as old as Ma Lily. Perhaps it was because he had never grown up mentally. I knew he was her brother without being told.

Young Jehu produced a clasp knife, opened a blade and sawed through a chunk of bread, holding the loaf against him and turning it as he cut. I chewed slowly as I watched him.

"'A use that knife for everything. Don't ye, Jehu?"

"Ay, gammer." He suddenly closed a massive hand round my wrist and pulled me towards the back door. Ma Lily chuckled and shook her head maternally, as if we were two children living in our own imaginary world.

We went out into a courtyard paved with flags. My caravan stood in an open-sided barn. Young Jehu led me past it and through a door in the rear wall. It took a moment for my eyes to become accustomed to the gloom. Then I saw Dobbin standing in a stall, chewing and smirking as usual. I thought at first that the rest of the barn was an aviary, but as shapes hardened I saw that the barn was a sort of studio filled with life-sized models. It was like looking into the hold of Noah's ark. Every type of bird was there, a pair of each, and beyond them were models of foxes and badgers and every type of rodent. In another quarter I saw domesticated animals: cows, sheep, pigs, horses, goats, dogs. The numbers were unbelievable. They filled the whole vast barn. At first I couldn't see what they were made of, then I realized they were all clay. But the strange thing about every one of them was that they all seemed to be straining to escape.

"Did you make them?" I asked and found I was whispering.

"They're my creation," Young Jehu nodded. "Look."

He took a piece of soft clay from a ledge and with a few deft movements drew a perfect feather on it with his knife. It looked so real that it might have floated down and settled there.

"They're waiting," Young Jehu said. He took a model of a small bird from his pocket and blew softly into its beak. It whistled so realistically that, if I'd not seen, I'd have sworn it was alive.

"What are they waiting for?" I asked.

"For you to free them."

I noticed he'd dropped all this "ye" business. I felt nervous.

"How can I do that?" I asked to humour him.

"Break her power."

"Whose?"

"Mother Lily's."

"I'll do that," I said to keep him happy.

Suddenly he grabbed my wrist again and it disappeared in his huge paw. He hauled me across the barn to a window. There was a field of corn outside.

"There you must do it."

"I will," I assured him, hoping that by agreeing, I'd be able to get away quickly. I don't mind admitting that holding hands in a bizarre natural history museum with a village idiot who seemed to have the strength of an ox brought out the latent coward in me.

"Break her and free my creatures," he repeated.

"I will," I promised. "You can rely on me."

He released me and stood staring out of the window as though he'd forgotten that I existed. I fled outside, back to the sunlight.

Evie came out of the kitchen door on the other side of the yard, obviously looking for me, and I forgot my panic.

"Oh, there ye be!" she exclaimed.

"Young Jehu's been showing me his collection."

"Well then, that mean 'a thinks ye be the chosen one."

"Me? Chosen for what?"

"To be the Green Man."

"What's that?"

She looked at me fondly, like a mother at a daft child. "One be chosen each year to accompany the Harvest Queen at the festivities," she explained patiently, laughing at my obtuseness.

"I can't be chosen. I don't live here," I protested, hoping she'd contradict me, so that then I would belong here.

"Oh, that don't matter none."

"Who chooses?"

"Ma Lily, of course."

"Then perhaps you're right and she's chosen me and told Young Jehu."

"'A allus knows. 'A don't need tellin' nothing."

112

"So I'm going to be the Green Man?" In spite of wanting to be part of the village, for some reason I didn't feel too happy about being this vegetable character. "That's why Young Jehu showed me his collection?"

"Ay, that be so. 'A shows the chosen one each year. No one else don't never go in there."

"Haven't you ever seen his models?"

"No fear. Ye wouldn't get me in there. Creepy place it be. Young Jehu's not like anyone else."

"You can say that again," I agreed.

"Besides, Ma Lily forbid anyone to go in there save the Green Man. She says it be Young Jehu's place and even 'a must have somewheres of his own."

"I see," I said, not seeing anything. "Let's go for a walk," I suggested, wanting to keep her to myself for as long as possible.

"This way," she said, and took my hand as though it was the most natural thing in the world. I tried to walk so that the front of my jeans looked flat.

"What happens at the harvest festivities?" I asked.

"Ye sees this field," she said. We were walking up the side of the field I'd seen from Young Jehu's window. I nodded. "This be the last field to be cut. 'Tis called Harvest Field and when 'tis done, there be a feast all night, and at midnight the Green Man ploughs the first furrow for the next year, so as there'll be a good crop."

"You mean I have to plough the field?" I asked, feeling alarmed.

"'Course ye do."

"I don't know how to drive a tractor."

"Oh, ye don't have to do nothing. They lads all take a rope apiece and haul on plough. Ye just guides it up the field to where I sits."

"What's your part, then?"

"Why, I be the Harvest Queen, ye girt lump. The Green Man be my husband, see. Us makes next year's harvest."

I suddenly felt enthusiastic about playing the part of the Green Man. You'll probably think me a romantic fool, but I started imagining staying in Ende for ever. Anything seemed possible there and, as I say, nothing appeared odd at the time. I felt I knew all these weird characters already, and I never made the connection with the myths I'd immersed myself in all my life. No one asked where I was from or what I was doing. I was just accepted as myself. And I'd done my reality test, hadn't I?

We went on up the track beside the field. I noticed that there were no fences or hedges. It was like medieval strip farming.

"Why aren't there any fences?" I asked.

"Why would we be wanting they?"

"I don't know," I laughed. The suggestion seemed foolish once I'd made it. Why would one need fences in a perfect world?

In other fields I could see men cutting the corn

with sickles. That didn't seem odd there, but it struck me I'd never seen it before, except in films.

"Why don't they use a combine?" I asked.

But we reached the top of the field and Evie didn't answer. In front of us, set in a semicircle of oak trees, was a stone chair. It was covered in carvings of fruit and vegetables rather as the Green Man on the inn sign was made up of them. A large, flat slab was set in the ground with grooves to channel rain into the field.

"This be where I sits," Evie told me, "and ye comes up the field to bring new life to the land. Do ye see?"

She looked openly at me. I pulled her to me and kissed her. She didn't resist. We slipped to the ground and lay surrounded by the browning wheat. We made love quite naturally. She swept away all the sex stuff my head was normally filled with. She was so pure, somehow, and innocent. I don't mean she said, No, I mustn't, and so on. It was as if what she was doing was natural, like an animal, free, without hang-ups or cares or worries. And I had none either.

I'd come home at last. This was where I belonged. Everything here was pure and natural and unpolluted. Just as I had always dreamed the world could be. Even my thoughts were wholesome.

We lay and looked at the sky.

"I wanted to get away from my world," I told her. "It's rotten. I was looking for somewhere like this, and for you."

"'Course ye were. And we were waiting for 'ee."

I was too interested in what I was feeling to pay much attention to her remarks.

"You know that if you rearrange the letters of Ende you can make Eden? Well, here I'm Adam and you're Eve."

"That's right, my old love. Ye remembers now."

"I'm going to stay here for ever."

"'Course ye are."

"It's too good to be true," I murmured. I was so moved by my vision that I wet her breasts with my tears.

All my dreams had come true. I was in love and loved in return. I had found a simple, pure world untainted by the corruption of my own.

The trouble with a dream, of course, is that it can turn into a nightmare before you know what's happening.

HARVEST MOON

I made love to Evie morning, noon and night in the days after that first time. She never said no. We always went to Harvest Field and afterwards we lay and by day watched the sun climb up the sky and by night watched the moon grow gradually larger.

"When's this festival?" I asked one day.

"When the moon be full," Evie answered as if it was obvious.

"No one's told me what I must do apart from this ploughing thing."

"Ye'll know when the time comes. Ye allus does."

If she said I'd know, then I'd know. I had perfect confidence in her.

I pushed all doubts behind me where they piled up like layers of snow. I could sense them there the way animals can sense an earthquake before it strikes. The hair on my neck sometimes prickled in anticipation of an avalanche. But my reality test had never yet failed me.

One morning, after I'd been there two weeks, Evie came bursting into my room.

"Get up, ye girt lie-a-bed!" she cried, laughing, and pulled the top pillow off me.

"What for?" I asked, fighting weakly and trying to grab her.

"They want 'ee to make first cut on Harvest Field."

I followed her downstairs and out into the courtyard. It was filled with the men I'd seen each day harvesting and each night drinking. They gave a cheer when I appeared.

One old boy in an unbuttoned waistcoat who seemed to be in charge, shouted, "Gie way for the Green Man, me lads."

They made a pathway across the yard towards Harvest Field. A young man thrust a sickle at me and leered. I felt that the implement was ancient. Its blade was rusted red and tiny figures were carved round its handle. My fingers traced the outline of their movements as they spiralled down to the blade. It seemed the carvings were telling a story but I could not sort out the sequence of events just then because hands were slapping me on the back and propelling me towards the stand of wheat.

I glanced back at the kitchen doorway, looking for Evie to give me guidance. Ma Lily stood there, smiling proudly, as though she'd been responsible for bringing me up and this was the moment when I set out to make my own way in the world. I felt that I mustn't let her down.

I crossed the road and halted at the edge of the field. The ears were golden but the stems were grey like steel bars. As I stood there I felt a chill in the air, the first touch of autumn, which made me shiver.

I was afraid that when I tried to use the sickle, all that would happen would be that I'd knock the stalks over. Still, I shrugged to myself. Evie had said it would be all right and I trusted her. It wasn't my fault if they chose someone from a town to be their Green Man. I held the sickle the way I'd seen them and got ready to swing.

As if that was the signal, they started to clap and the old boy chanted in time with the rhythm:

"Cut Harvest Field,
and bind the sheaves
and start the seasons round."

The clapping distracted me, and when I chopped at the corn I did so with an easy movement, not stiff with concentration. The stalks tumbled smoothly in succession as the sickle cut them from the ground. There was a cheer and then everyone set to work. The men with the sickles moved up the field in a staggered line and behind each came someone to bind the cut wheat into sheaves and stook them.

I watched for a bit before turning away. Someone had taken the sickle from me.

I went to say good morning to Dobbin. Young Jehu looked after him for me. Evie seemed to ignore the fact that he even existed. I thought she was nervous of horses, as she would walk all the way round the barn rather than cut through the passage next to Dobbin's stall.

When I arrived, Young Jehu had just dumped a load of hay in the stall and Dobbin was chewing contentedly.

"Harvest Moon tonight," Young Jehu said.

"Looking forward to the festivities?" I asked, patronizing the village idiot.

"It's you or her. Remember that." He wagged his misshapen head at me.

"I'll remember," I assured him solemnly, edging away. Somehow he disturbed my perfect world. He threatened to bring down the avalanche.

"The Mother must be fed."

I cleared off to the warmth of the kitchen.

I didn't see much of Evie that day. She and Ma Lily and other women were busy baking for the feast. I wandered about watching the harvesters work their way up the field towards the stone chair and the runnelled slab in front of it.

They came to the flattened place where we made love and passed a lot of lewd remarks which annoyed me, because it wasn't like that.

The old boy said, "'Tis thy duty, Green Man.

Don't harken to they."

"Aye, that's right," another added. "Gie it to her hot and strong."

"The old Green Man did us proud," one of them said and the others agreed.

"This be the finest harvest in memory," the old one confirmed.

"'A did his duty, no denying."

"So at her agin, Green Man," they told me.

I didn't know how to answer them. To have a lot of men telling you to make love to one of their village girls is something you've never been prepared for. It was odd, too, I thought even then, that no local lad was after her.

I pushed it all behind me because Evie was everything to me. She was the sun by day and her nearness made my skin glow, and she was the stars by night and her touch made my senses tingle. She overwhelmed me. I was hers without reserve. I had found someone free of the attitudes and physical imperfections which destroyed other girls' desirability.

The day they cut Harvest Field was the first since I'd been there that I didn't spend almost every waking moment with Evie. She managed to slip away in the afternoon to be with me, and I laid my head on her breast and wept again, as I had the first time. I was choked by joy.

"Life is going to go on like this for ever," I told her.

"Of course it is," she assured me, stroking my hair.

I was trying desperately not to look over my shoulder, but I was increasingly aware of the avalanche looming behind me.

By evening the field was cut and the sheaves gathered. In the courtyard, trestle-tables, laid out in a horseshoe, were laden with food and jugs of beer and cider. I was looking forward to the celebration: it would keep my mind safely occupied. Also I was thinking about later on when Evie and I would be alone.

We sat at the head of the table under an arch of sheaves tied onto a wooden frame. There was a deafening uproar from people shouting, laughing, drinking and playing on a flute and drum which was a hollowed out log. The harvest moon lit the scene.

When it finally got dark a bonfire was lit and by its light a sort of morris dance was performed. The repetitive weaving of the dancers hypnotized me and I felt giddy. I'd drunk a bit but not enough to stop me seeing that all their movements, and the gestures they made with their quarterstaves, had sexual meanings. The buffoon who ran about among the spectators playing simple-minded tricks made the meaning clear, if anyone hadn't got it already. When he came in front of us he mimed crudely our actions in the Harvest Field.

"Who was Harvest Queen last year?" I don't know why I asked Evie that just then. I felt it was a question I should push behind me, and I wished I had when she answered.

"Why, I was, of course. Ye remember." She laughed, watching the dancers.

My stomach gave a lurch and I felt sick. I took a drink and hid my face behind a great earthenware tankard. Images of Evie giving herself to someone else forced themselves into my imagination.

"Was it like this year?" I couldn't stop myself asking.

"It were the best year ever," she told me. "Look at harvest."

"How many times," I asked, not wanting to know, "have you been Harvest Queen?"

"I don't know," she laughed. "Too many to count."

Pure, innocent, fresh, clean, free from pollution, I thought bitterly. No wonder no one was jealous of me. She was a bitch on heat, the village whore. I wanted to kill her, or myself. I drained my tankard and filled it again. The avalanche descended and things became blurred by drink or tears.

"'Tis time," Evie whispered. "Ye'll come again next year?" she asked.

I thought I was going mad. Did she really think I was the same Green Man as last time?

She slipped away and I watched her, hating her and wanting her to come back and deny it, even if it was true.

Ma Lily stood at the bottom of Harvest Field

and gave her the ancient sickle, then Evie headed for her stone throne. As she took the sickle, it was as though I held it again as I had that morning and in memory I found I could run my fingers over each figure on the handle and read the story as it ran down to the blade.

There was a man who rose from the ground and was made of all the fruits of the earth. The Harvest Queen was given to him for a season and the next year's harvest was the blessing he bestowed and price he paid for his brief marriage. For at the end of the Harvest Festival he returned to the earth and made it fruitful.

Then I remembered the sign outside the inn with the sickle cutting the Green Man's sheaf-legs from beneath him, and the red rust stain on the sickle blade, and I realized that the grooves on the slab in front of the Harvest Queen's throne were not for rain. I knew without a flicker of doubt that I was to be sacrificed on her altar-stone with the ancient sickle and that my blood would feed the valley.

The old boy who'd led the harvesters this morning suddenly stood up and began to bang his tankard stolidly on the wooden trestle in front of him. The whole party gradually picked up the rhythm. It was slow, like a funeral drum. Then the flute started, weaving a pattern in and out of the thumping. Next the harvesters began to stamp their feet, clogs on cobbles. Lastly the old boy raised his voice in their harvest anthem:

"There were three men rose out of the west,
Their fortunes for to try,
And they three men did solemnly vow
John Barleycorn should die.
They ploughed, they sowed, they hoed him in,
Rained clods upon his head,
And they three men did solemnly vow
John Barleycorn were dead."

They roared the ancient verses, telling the story of their lives. It was the climax of their year.

The beat seemed to strike in time with my pulse and the flute made my head spin. I looked round helplessly. The merry harvesters I'd come to love because they were different to everyone else were working themselves up to murder. In the firelight their faces were brutal and soul-less.

I searched the scene for a way to escape. Suddenly I saw Young Jehu hovering on the outskirts of the festivities. He looked more demented than ever.

He must have felt my eyes on him because he jerked his head up sharply and beckoned me with his huge hand. I pushed my way round to him, bumping into shapes which reeled out of the wavering shadows.

Young Jehu's face was running with sweat and his eyes were wide open like a startled animal's.

"Now's your time," he panted. "Before they come for you."

He took hold of me and dragged me through the

gap in the building which led to his barn. I glimpsed Ma Lily's alarmed face across the far side of the courtyard. But I followed Young Jehu. He was my only fragile hope.

Rounding the barn the full moon froze the scene before me. We were at the bottom of Harvest Field. Waiting there was Dobbin, hitched to a plough, and halfway up the field was Evie with the sickle in her hand.

"You must break the soil with a plough pulled by your beast."

I started to ask why, but Young Jehu just looped the reins over my shoulders and knotted them to the plough handle.

"Break the earth and break the Mother," he chanted in my ear. "The land must have blood. Yours or hers."

I believed him then, but I didn't understand.

Young Jehu suddenly pulled out his shut-knife and opening the blade plunged it into Dobbin's flank. The blade was in to the hilt and out again before I could protest. Then it was too late to speak.

The horse lunged forward with a scream and the reins fastened round my shoulders dragged me with it. To keep my balance I grabbed the plough handles and my weight drove the blade into the ground. I stumbled up the field, helplessly doing as Young Jehu had instructed.

At Dobbin's shriek, Evie turned. In the moonlight the scene was clear. She dropped the sickle and ran towards me.

"Not that way," she was shouting. "'Tis wrong so. 'Tis wrong."

Then the horror happened – and I delighted in it.

Evie came running down the field towards me, and it was as though in looking at me she didn't see Dobbin. She collided with him and flew backwards, her arms and legs flung outwards. Spread-eagled, she lay in my path. I couldn't have stopped Dobbin even if I'd wanted, and one part of me didn't want to.

The blade of the plough sliced forward between her legs cutting her in two. And even while it was happening, I thought bitterly, no one else will plough your furrow. That was the worst horror. Not killing her, but the discovery that such a thought could come from my mind. Then. Even while it was happening, I thought of sex. Until that moment I hadn't really known how degenerate I was.

Dobbin dragged me to the top of the field and stopped at the stone seat. The tip of the plough rested on the flat slab in front of it. Blood ran off the blade, down the channels and into the earth. Not mine. But I wished that it was. I fought to free myself from the reins. I was going to go back to Evie.

In the distance I could hear the tapping of the drum. It seemed to pound in my head. I was terrified. The whole moonlit scene had come alive. The

127

trees, the plough, the stone seat, even the earth itself flung themselves at me faster and faster as the rhythm of the drum increased. I was paralyzed, tied to the plough and anchored to the stone slab like a sacrificial victim. My executioner was dead but the valley itself demanded vengeance.

Then Young Jehu was there, grinning wildly, the sickle in his huge hand. He brandished it above my head. My eyes closed. I heard the swish of the blade. My stomach melted, and I thought that it had split me in two just like Evie. Then the tangled reins fell apart and I was free.

Young Jehu lifted me in one arm and dragged me through the circle of oak trees onto a track. In front of me stood my caravan with Dobbin harnessed between the shafts. Young Jehu dumped me on the step and slapped Dobbin with a crack like a whip. The horse obediently took up his resigned plod.

I was so relieved to be alive that all I could do was clutch at whatever my hand touched. I clung to the edge of the door and tried to dig my fingers into it in case it should turn into a dream and disappear.

I looked back through the massive trunks of the sacred grove. Young Jehu was leaping about on the stone seat and twirling the sickle in murderous circles above his head in an ungainly victory dance. With his huge ears and shapeless mouth he looked so inbred that I had the conviction that he had created himself.

I looked down the field. Stumbling over the stubble came Ma Lily shrieking her horror at what had happened. With each circle of the sickle Young Jehu seemed to grow stronger while Ma Lily shrank.

Young Jehu took something from his pocket and put it to his wet lips. I saw it was his bird whistle. But this time, when he blew, it didn't just sing, it stretched its wings and flew away crying its release. At the same time, from his barn at the bottom of the field, came a noise as though every creature in creation had shrilled in unison. Then the doors burst open and Young Jehu's animals swarmed out and stampeded up the field.

Ma Lily threw up her hands in an attempt to halt them, or in despair. But they swept over her, and when they'd passed, she had gone. I looked again, but she had melted into the earth. I realized for the first time that since I'd been in the valley I had never heard a bird or seen an animal, and I'd not eaten eggs or butter or meat.

Then I heard Young Jehu crying, "The Mother is broken. The Mother is broken."

The last thing I remember is sitting slumped on the step of the caravan while Dobbin dragged me up the track which led out of the valley. I was mumbling, "Get thee to a nunnery. Get thee to a nunnery," over and over. It's what Hamlet says to his girl Ophelia after he's realized the whole world's corrupt. I don't know who I was saying it to.

LIMBO

What I want to know is, do I have to write down what happened after I emerged from Ende? Since then I've had all the bounce of a deflated balloon. But my psychiatrist insists, and since she can't cross her legs without flashing her thighs, I agree. Just for her. Sorry, a slip of the tongue. As she keeps reminding me, I'm writing this for my own benefit, not hers.

I left the valley without being aware of doing so. The next thing I knew, it seemed to be about mid-morning and I was lolling on the step of the caravan. At some point Dobbin and I had found our way onto a regular road.

The trees were like pantomime scenery behind a gossamer curtain. I felt as woozy as the morning after my attempt to drown myself. Perhaps it *was* the next morning. How long had the Ende episode lasted? Well, put it this way: how long's a hallucination, a reality gap, a piece of string?

I tried to clear my thoughts by focusing on Dobbin's arse which, on account of some leaves stuck to it, looked like one of those sideways smiley computer faces. Ende still seemed real to me, like a dream injury that throbs after you've woken up. I couldn't at first accept that it had all been the product of my own febrile mind.

"How long since…?" I tried to ask Dobbin, but I wasn't sure what event to choose as my anchor in real time.

I was still searching my memory for some solid ground when a police car, like Mercury, the gods' winged messenger, squeezed between the van and the trees.

"Here's the answer," I said to Dobbin.

The car stopped in the middle of the road about half a mile ahead, as though Dobbin were an oil-tanker and needed twenty times his own length to halt.

A male and a female uniform climbed slowly out of the car. They donned headgear. I was pleased to note this dedication to regulation dress.

I had a momentary flicker of a hallucination, like the faint memory of a past life, and I saw them leaning on their car cradling shotguns. Was I wanted for the murder of Evie? I wondered. Get a grip on reality, I told myself. You're suffering from a surfeit of American movies.

That made me think of Lois and Dad. I wondered what legal landslide I'd brought down on

Mum and Jake. I suddenly felt queasy. Could it be a twinge of conscience? I wasn't sure, not being familiar with the sensation.

Dobbin plodded up to the cops and halted smartly, as though he had always cherished the ambition to be a police horse and wanted to make a good impression.

"Good morning, sir," the policeman said with a practised lack of sincerity. He admired my refurbished van. "What have we here?" he asked rhetorically.

"Mobile incident room," I told him. "Camouflaged. Do you have any of that pretty blue and white plastic ribbon? Oh, and some chalk. I'll draw a silhouette on the road and we can get started."

But my heart wasn't in it. I was going through the motions from force of habit.

"Would you be Michael Jester?" he asked stoically, not being allowed to respond in kind.

I had another twinge of conscience. I also felt I wasn't going to be able to continue balancing on the step for much longer.

The policewoman came up alongside me. She stopped with her foot in front of the wheel as if to prevent Dobbin making a dash for it. I used my remaining strength to put the brake on. She was young and plump. Policewomen look plumper every day.

"Shall I take the reins for you?" she asked pleasantly.

They dropped from my fingers and fell across her arms like party streamers.

She had wonderfully comforting breasts, I observed as I toppled off the step towards them.

"I'll come quietly," I punned, as I attempted to lay my head on her bosom.

She wrapped her arms round me and staggered backwards into Dobbin.

The air was filled with the scent of pine resin from the trees, but I thought it emanated from her.

"You'd better call an ambulance," she told her colleague, panting under my weight.

I couldn't feel my legs and I was aware of sliding down her. I heard an echo of the call her companion was transmitting.

"Do you have an underwired bra?" I tried to ask. "Your diaphragm's receiving messages."

"Get a blanket out of the car," she said, rather impatiently, I thought.

She attempted to lay me down in the road, but my hair caught in the clip which fastened her radio to her pullover.

"For Christ's sake, come and help me," she snapped.

I drifted into oblivion.

Sometime later I regained consciousness in a hospital bed. I was dressed in a garment which was unidentifiable and made of glass paper. At least I'd broken the habit of waking up naked.

For a moment I thought I was still lying in the road next to the caravan because my eyes opened on a view of green vegetable matter. I blinked several times and grapes floated tantalizingly into focus.

My mouth tasted of chemicals but I seemed to have lost the ability to control my limbs and I couldn't reach them. Eventually a nurse floated into view above me. By coincidence, she had grapes in her bra.

"Lower," I croaked.

"Oh, you're awake, are you?" she asked rhetorically.

"Does a nurse called Anna work here?" I tried to ask.

"If you feel like being sick, use the bowl," she told me deafly.

Hours, days or weeks passed. It was difficult to tell. Visitors merged into dreams. Mum clasped my hand to her breasts and gazed nobly, but she left on a unicorn.

At last I got bored with introspection and instead studied my fingernails, which had grown.

A nurse came and lifted a wrist with a hand so cool no depravity would ever infect it. "You're discharged," she announced to her watch.

"Wonderful," I confided. "I always welcome a discharge." But it was force of habit.

"There's nothing the matter with you that an expensive psychiatrist can't put right," she informed me with professional callousness. "Your own doctor will make an appointment for you."

When I got home, Jake III was no more. Dad

and Lois had unleashed the dogs of the law and Mum and he had parted under the strain. I definitely felt a pang of conscience. I tried to salve it by telling myself that he wouldn't have lasted, neither of the other Jakes had. But then, I had always been the fly in the ointment.

One evening, when I'd been back a few days and had all my faculties under my command, I tried to apologize to Mum. We were in the sitting-room. I was on the settee, Mum was admiring the gilt mirror above the fireplace. It seemed a suitably intimate moment to try to move our relationship on to a more mature level.

"Mum, I'm sorry about Jake," I started to say.

She fluffed her hair and sighed bravely. "Jake never understood the bonds between a mother and son."

"No, Mum, and I've not understood the bonds between a mother and a stepfather," I tried to confess.

But she rolled over me: "We don't need anyone else, do we? You're Mummy's champion, like always, aren't you?"

"I was trying to say, I think I've grown up a bit."

"We'll face the world together," she said, gazing at the mirror.

I gave up. "Yes, Mum. Whatever you say." It takes two to tango.

"I'm going to have a complete makeover," she decided, looking at one profile, then the other.

*　　*　　*

The opportunity to test my newly minted maturity occurred a few weeks later. I was stretched out reading a textbook when the front door closed and after a longer-than-usual pause Mum appeared coyly in the doorway to the sitting-room. My scalp prickled in conditioned reflex, but I couldn't identify the stimulus for a minute.

"There's someone I want you to meet, Michael," she said, and came into the room revealing a figure behind her. Then she delivered her killer introduction: "I'm sure we're all going to get on really well."

Guess who? The prize is a used car. Yes, it was Jake IV.

I said I was pleased to meet him. He saw the A-level book and asked what I was going to do when I left school.

"I want to study law," I said.

"There's money in that game," he told Mum, and winked to make me an accomplice.

Well, call me a sentimental schmuck if you like, but I've resolved to do what I can to make the path to alimony as long as possible.

While I do, I've got my psychiatrist to keep me amused, or vice versa. She is so understanding and non-judgmental I could plead provocation if I committed an atrocity. I amuse myself, though, by lacing my sessions with mythical archetypes. She particularly likes those she discovers in tales of my Ende trip. The idea of a perfect existence in a place ruled over by Lilith the earth mother, as she calls

Lily, and her struggle with the all-conquering sky god Jehu, or Jehovah, are her particular favourites. She is also keen on fertility rituals starring John Barleycorn. What she wants me to do is see how they relate to my life. Well, anything to oblige, since they get her crossing and recrossing her legs. She's very young.

The result is, as you guessed, this account might be true or it might not. I sometimes see myself as the archetypal Jester. Do psychiatrists have a sense of humour? Whatever. Miss Frisson might see this account or she might not. I've not decided yet.

In conclusion, I should like to make it clear to all my fans that I am definitely not using drugs any more. Not socially, recreationally, unintentionally. That's it. Absolutely. Finito. For ever – or until the next time, anyway. No – no. Just my little jest. Force of habit.

SPRING ARCHETYPE

I've met Anna again.

She turned up at The Cottage in the Easter holidays. It seems I told her about the wrought-iron lobster pot on the wall, and she wandered around until she found it.

"I wondered if you were all right," she said after I'd invited her in for a coffee.

We sat at the kitchen table and I studied her. The first time I'd seen her by daylight. She's got a quizzical smile, lopsided.

"What I need is a personal nurse," I told her.

"I was worried because I knew you'd taken some of Karen's pills," she said seriously. "I hoped at the time it was just E, but there was this huge crisis at the hospital and everything came out. It seems that Karen and some others were using Ativan and anything they could get hold of from the pharmacy. And it wasn't E they were taking with everything else, it was MDEA."

"I don't know that."

"Instead of making you sociable it takes you inside yourself."

The letters clicked. "Medea was a nasty piece of work, mythically speaking," I said.

"Dad didn't tell me her story."

"Probably because she killed her own kids."

"Good name for her, then."

"What happened to Karen?"

"She became psychotic. Spent four months in the psychiatric unit."

"I'm not surprised," I said, deciding to spare her the chore of explaining psychotic. I've looked it up since and it means suffering from illusions, hallucinations, delusions and mental confusion. (Hello, Karen. Fancy meeting you here.)

"Now she's a Born Again Christian," Anna said, turning down the corners of her mouth.

"Some people can't live without drugs."

"She's a reformed character, unbearably priggish. We don't see much of each other any more."

"You two didn't seem much alike."

Mum came in just then.

"Oh, I didn't know you had anyone with you," she lied, giving Anna the once-over.

I introduced them. "We met last summer," I explained.

A slight frown pinched Mum's forehead.

"Last summer," she repeated, like someone who didn't want her amnesia disturbed.

"We were just going out," I said.

Anna and I strolled down to the stone jetty and hung over the parapet. There was a cold wind and no holidaymakers. The waves moved sluggishly, as if their specific gravity were greater than usual.

"Did we really come here after the club?" I asked.

Anna nodded. "We paddled and ran along the sand. Oh, and we listened to Cerberus."

"I was thinking of giving up mythology," I told her in passing. "I got a bit too involved in it and I wasn't sure what was real." I paused. "You know, when I left you at your guest-house, did you get undressed in front of your window? Without drawing the curtains, I mean."

"Acting out your fantasies would cost you more than two drinks."

"That's what I thought."

I told her what I'd imagined I'd seen.

"I'm pretty sure I drank Karen's pint, and I seem to remember her dropping a prescription's worth of capsules in it. I didn't think about it at the time. And there was some guy with something on blotting-paper which I suppose leeched into my skin."

"It sounds like you had even more than her," Anna said, "but since you weren't used to it, the effect was probably stronger. Karen had been taking anything she could get hold of for ages." She shrugged helplessly. "I'd guess your mental state before you took it would also affect your reaction."

"Thanks a lot," I said. Then I cheered up. "I think I'm back to normal," I confessed. "In fact, I'm more normal than I've ever been."

"And there was me making allowances for the Ativan," she said, trying to look worried.

I like Anna's mouth, now, even though it is lop-sided. No. I like it because it is lopsided.

We're going to go on seeing each other. I don't know what I expect from her – or she from me – but something more than the obvious which imme-diately springs to mind. I suppose I want her to make everything worthwhile. Is that asking too much of one person? Anyway, when I'm with her I feel that there is more to life than used cars. There is, isn't there?

I hope.